SARAH SUMNER HAS BRILLIANTLY CAPTURED THE HEART OF WHAT IT TAKES TO BE A GREAT LEADER . . . and where and why many of us fall short. The People Model provides readers unique insights into our individual personality styles, what traits truly work for us, which ones don't, and most importantly, what we need to do if we aspire to become what we were created to be. Her ability to incorporate spiritual truths in a modern-day format is especially distinctive. I strongly encourage anyone who wants to be a more effective leader and lead a more personally fulfilled life to read this book . . . it is life changing!

RICHARD ANDERSEN
Executive Vice President
San Diego Padres Park

The People Model is an excellent tool kit for everyday usage, whether in business or social settings. The self-awareness it creates is refreshing, powerful, and meaningful. After reading *Leadership above the Line*, you'll be motivated and prepared to hone your style for greater effectiveness.

MIKE HUGHES
Senior Vice President
Safeco Insurance

Sarah Sumner's People Model is a valuable contribution to the literature on leadership. While many books on the subject acknowledge the importance of self-awareness, this one offers a useful tool for actually achieving it. She presents her concept in an understandable and highly readable format that will engage almost any reader.

JOHN C. KNAPP
President
The Southern Institute for Business and Professional Ethics
Senior Scholar and Professor of Ethical Leadership
Kennesaw State University

Leadership above the Line provides a thought-provoking and practical approach that can be applied in virtually any organization. It helps managers better understand personal leadership styles and avoid "below the line" tendencies that may undermine leadership effectiveness. I highly recommend this book. It can lead to constructive dialogue among those already in leadership, as well as train and develop future leaders.

LUELLEN LUCID
Global Quality Leader, Human Capital Group
Watson Wyatt & Company

IF YOU LEAD LEADERS, PUSH OTHER BOOKS ASIDE—AND MAKE THIS THE NEXT ONE YOU READ. *Leadership above the Line* is 60 percent story, 100 percent breakthrough insights on leadership formation. Dr. Sarah Sumner's character-based model is clear, her story is compelling, and her application tools are transformational. Highly recommended!

DAVID SANFORD
President
Sanford Communications, Inc.

Do you lead? Do you work with leaders? Do you want to be a leader? Then get a firm grip on the People Model and gain a better understanding of what drives people to make decisions, whether good or bad. Learn from it. Grow with it. You'll be glad you did.

JAMES M. STOCKHAM
Director of Marketing, Category Management and Field Sales
Farmer John (Clougherty Packing, LLC)

The ancient philosophical categories of truth, beauty, and goodness find a fresh flowering of relevance in the inspired hands of Dr. Sarah Sumner. Serious attention to the People Model will result in better people and better organizations. Her metaphor of operating "above the line" is becoming my favorite for describing sound ethics applied in the hard-scrabble realities of modern life. Dr. Sumner offers us not only a worthy *end*—character in leadership—but also a *means* for developing it.

LARRY R. DONNITHORNE
Author
The West Point Way of Leadership: From Learning Principled Leadership to Practicing It

---

Leadership above the Line is a great book to give friends and colleagues. It offers profound insights into the behaviors, motives, and fears associated with different leadership styles. You'll recognize immediately the value that this book will bring on a day-to-day basis. I've embraced the model and already achieved positive results.

JANICE TROEGER
Director
Clinical Planning and Operations, Medication Delivery
Baxter Healthcare
Board of Directors, Willow Creek Community Church

DR. SARAH SUMNER

LEADERSHIP ABOVE THE LINE

TYNDALE HOUSE PUBLISHERS, INC.

CAROL STREAM, ILLINOIS

Visit Tyndale's exciting Web site at www.tyndale.com

TYNDALE and Tyndale's quill logo are registered trademarks of Tyndale House Publishers, Inc.

Leadership above the Line

Copyright © 2006 by Sarah Sumner. All rights reserved.

Designed by Dean H. Renninger

Library of Congress Cataloging-in-Publication Data

Sumner, Sarah, date.
  Leadership above the line / Sarah Sumner.
    p. cm.
  ISBN-13: 978-1-4143-0573-8 (hc)
  ISBN-10: 1-4143-0573-7 (hc)
  1. Leadership. I. Title.
  BF637.L4S88 2006
  158'.4—dc22   2006003732

Printed in the United States of America

12 11 10 09 08 07 06
7   6   5   4   3   2   1

DEDICATION

*To Kimberley Wiedefeld,
apart from whom this book
would not exist*

CONTENTS

FOREWORD

This is a timely book. The great cry today is for leadership formation, for the creation of a foolproof process that will ensure leadership success and shield growing organizations from leadership failure. The only problem is that this cry continues to go largely unheeded. Dr. Sarah Sumner, however, has a passion to see character-centered leadership flourish within every organization, and her book offers a fresh, insightful perspective on this topic. Several years ago I had the privilege of hiring Dr. Sumner when I was at Azusa Pacific University. Since then, Sarah has gone on to distinguish herself as an able scholar, a profound teacher, and an impressive minister. Her insatiable appetite for learning is reflected throughout these pages, as is her desire for excellence.

In *Leadership above the Line*, Sarah introduces us to the People Model and offers a parable that shows how leadership develops.

In the midst of this model, we see real personalities spring to life, wrestling not so much with principles, but with the competing priorities of real leadership in real time with real consequences.

So many leadership books go one of two directions: either offering a didactic message that appeals to the hyperrational mind or offering a narrative approach that tugs on our emotions. The appeal of Sarah's book is that it reaches out to both mind-sets. She opens the book by offering a descriptive model to which she gives flesh and bones a few pages later. In the opening section, Sarah defines not only the principles, but also the realities that exist in every organization.

It is in this opening that we are invited to recognize that people think and act differently. No immediate value decision is made, only a simple acknowledgment that this is the way the world works and that every person not only has multiple sides to his or her personality, but also a dominant and preferred approach. These innate tendencies guide our decisions and our participation in every organization we join. The beauty of this point is its amplification of a key theme circulating in much contemporary leadership literature: A person's instincts are central to his or her decision making.

In developing the People Model, Sarah used the three dominant archetypes of truth, goodness, and beauty, reflecting the influence of the ancient Greeks, and these archetypes guide the remainder of the book. We all have an innate sense of truth, goodness, and beauty; we just have it in different amounts and express it in different ways.

The personalities in the parable that amplify the model and form the heart of the book could be taken from any organization. Each of the five featured individuals displays character qualities we have seen in others and at times have even seen in ourselves. To help us understand these tendencies, Sarah concludes the book with several tools that unveil our tendencies personally and organizationally. These tools are meant to be suggestive, not conclusive, and their biggest role is to prod us to think about the attitudes and behaviors that dominate our interaction with colleagues and, in turn, reflect our deepest commitments.

One of the biggest challenges in any organization is to gain self-awareness as individual employees and as a company. This is often a threatening process because it reveals not only our strengths, but also the areas where we remain insufficient. But Sarah's book is helpful at just this point as it prompts us to gain self-awareness while providing tools to help us undergo the change and transformation that will make us more effective.

In Jim Collins's book *Good to Great,* he explains that what separates those outstanding executives who lead their companies to greatness from those top-notch executives whose companies never reach (or remain at) the top is this: The former strive to serve the larger mission of their organization, while the others work hard to serve their own ego needs. In many respects, Sarah is challenging us to lay aside our dominant egos for the greater good of the organization, inviting all parties to the table to gain a deeper understanding of our companies and work together to build a redemptive community that manifests the love of Christ. Although this book is written primarily as a crossover book for leaders in all organizations, it cannot be overlooked that a key to all successful leadership is to guide from a foundation anchored to Jesus Christ. This is a priority introduced at the end, but a theme that undergirds the entire project.

As you begin to read and enjoy this book, keep one final thought in mind. We are not born fully formed. We must develop. This book is meant to stimulate such development. Not one of us is ever beyond growing or needing to acquire new skills, abilities, and understandings. This reality is driven home by the very open-ended nature of the story. Although the story has a conclusion, it is not the end of the story, but only a new beginning for the individuals who make up this mythical company. This myth is reality. Every new level of self-awareness and corporate awareness begins a whole new cycle of growth and development. To this end we should be grateful for the work of Dr. Sumner, who amplifies this reality and in turn provides possibilities for our own improvement in such an attractive and appealing way. May your own life and leadership be enriched.

Gayle D. Beebe, PhD
PRESIDENT
SPRING ARBOR UNIVERSITY
THANKSGIVING 2005

PART ONE

THE
MODEL

CHAPTER 1

ABOUT THE
PEOPLE MODEL

This is a book about people. It's a book about building good character and *leading* from good character. It's a book designed for people who are ready to get serious about developing into first-rate leaders. It's also meant for leaders who are doggedly determined to solidify first-rate teams.

Almost all of us agree that good character is the centerpiece of authentic first-rate leadership. Good character is the key to good leadership because people tend to follow whatever standard the leader sets. Recent studies in moral intelligence show that the level of morality exercised by a company's character consistently affects the bottom line. It takes good character to grapple with reality. It takes good character to treat people right. It takes good character to build unity among networks of people and causes.

Thus every situation that a leader might face calls for the same three attributes: humility, courage, and honesty.

Most leaders have the willingness to improve their character, but so often they are not told how to do so. How do leaders learn to lead "above the line," so to speak? How can leaders grow in self-awareness? How can leaders learn to look inwardly? How can they keep themselves from becoming too defensive to accept the kind of feedback that they need?

These questions are important because people are important. Moreover, as research studies show, character deficits lead to financial deficits in the long run. Character deficits are very costly. Qualities such as arrogance and presumption, cowardice and people pleasing, deception and image management all weigh companies down.

Of course, no leader *wants* to lead with character deficits. Yet everyone has seen character deficits play out. I have seen them play out in various studies that I conducted while earning my MBA. I have seen them play out in magazine and newspaper articles. I have seen them in my places of employment. Most vividly I have seen them in myself.

Though by vocation I work in a private university, I wrote this book for people in a variety of fields. My primary target audience is the business community, yet the book applies to anyone in any setting—including nonprofit organizations, churches, and even families.

The uniqueness of this book is that it teaches through an instrument called the People Model. Take note: The People Model is based on Greek philosophy, yet it is original in its form and application. Like other innovations, it began as intuition. It was born from a hunch that burst into a full-blown model because logic gave it structure and meaning. Though the People

Model is not scientific or research based, it's empirical in the sense that experience confirms its validity. Essentially it's a grid that describes three sets of people: the Strategists, the Humanitarians, and the Diplomats. But the model is much more than a grid.

The People Model is a tool that can be used for practical purposes: to increase self-awareness, to make sense of confusing situations, to motivate people, to instigate changes, to establish stronger teams, to imagine new solutions, and to approach hard conversations more effectively. The People Model presents such a fresh way of thinking that its fruitfulness is hard to exhaust.

Another way of putting it is that the People Model yields three discrete types of decision-making power: *explanatory power* to interpret organizational behavior, *motivational power* to muster up people's willingness to forfeit stubborn habits that have weakened their effectiveness in the past, and *creative power* to imagine wise solutions for the future.

The birth of the People Model was intentional in the sense that I was trying to crack a code. I was trying to make sense of confusing situations I had personally observed over the years. I also was trying to learn more and better ways to respond to sticky issues in the workplace. I started my reflections—at least on a conscious level—with the premise that people usually do things for a reason; we operate from specific motivations. What the People Model shows is that those reasons and motivations sometimes can dramatically clash.

After reflecting deeply, I realized that the hardest lessons I've learned about leadership have come to me in the context of complex situations. What the People Model shows is that difficult situations can't be fairly sorted out simply by dubbing some people as "good guys" and others as "bad guys." While it's true the world has its tyrants and its heroes, it is also true that tyrants have their good points and that heroes aren't heroic in every way.

Although the People Model itself came to me as a blast of inspiration, it only took one evening for me to see it playing out in every workplace I've been part of and every relationship I've been in. For example, I could see it in my marriage. I could see it in my family, my workplace, my church, and in every organization that I knew of. That's why I have named it the People Model. Wherever people are, the model is there as well.

To be clear, the People Model applies both to individuals and organizations. Though every person and every company is a mix of all three types, there's a test that you can use informally to help you see which category most closely mirrors you. You can also use this test to assess your organization as a whole. If you want, you can take the test (beginning on page 173) now.

Okay, on to the model. My intention is to present it in three ways: (a) by explaining its basic form, (b) by illustrating its implications through a fictional story, and (c) by describing different ways to apply it. These three presentations are respectively reflected in the structure of the book.

Part 1 gives the bare bones of the model. Part 2 shows in detail how the model plays out and elaborates on its endless implications. Part 3 deals with practical application, putting the model to use. Part 4 includes a test and a workbook. Though the workbook is designed for small group discussion, you can use it privately if you like. Since the People Model applies to virtually every situation, you as the reader are left to decide how deep you want to go in your self-examination and assessment of your team or organization.

Now let's dive in and see what kind of impact the People Model has on you.

CHAPTER 2

THREE BASIC SETS OF STRENGTHS

According to the People Model, each person tends to think, solve problems, and interact with others in one of three main ways. Some are inclined to think in terms of truth, some in terms of goodness, and some in terms of beauty. These three ways of thinking are reflective of Plato's philosophical ideals: the True, the Good, and the Beautiful. However, since people don't consciously make decisions in terms of truth, goodness, and beauty, it isn't very helpful to name the three groups with Plato's words. Instead, I have labeled the three groups the Strategists, the Humanitarians, and the Diplomats.

The first group is called the Strategists because people in this category primarily tend to think in terms of truth and reality. They feel ill at ease when truth is covered up or misrepresented. To them, it feels strategic—not uncomfortable—to ask hard questions and face difficult problems head-on. The second group, the Humanitarians, is labeled as such because people in this category primarily tend to think in terms of goodness and humanity. They feel unsettled when people are devalued or hurt. To them, it seems imperative—not optional—to care about people and develop them. The third group is called the Diplomats because people in this category primarily tend to think in terms of beauty (that is, perceptions) and public relations. They feel bothered when peace and public order are violated. To them, it feels perfectly natural—not contrived—to unify factions and add a creative touch to the way things look.

To be clear, I am not saying that Strategists are strategic, and Humanitarians and Diplomats are not. Nor am I suggesting that the Humanitarians are people oriented, and Diplomats and Strategists are not. Nor am I saying that Diplomats are diplomatic, and Strategists and Humanitarians are not. What I'm saying is that each type has a tendency to prioritize a particular set of values. I am also saying that while everyone is a mix of all three types, each person has a tendency to lean toward one of the three. Yet all three ways of thinking are vital to the success of an organization.

Now for the framework of the People Model. If I had a piece of paper, I would begin by drawing two vertical lines to divide a blank sheet of paper into thirds. I would then write *Strategists* at the top of the first column on the left. In parentheses, I would write the word *light*.

Metaphorically speaking, Strategists shed light in the com-

STRATEGISTS (Light)		

pany. They like to bring the facts out into the open. They tend to deal with problems head-on. As light heals, so truth heals. As light exposes things that are hidden in the dark, so truth uncovers facts. Truth sets people free. When the company values truth-telling, then people who tell the truth are rewarded for being honest. They're listened to and respected, even solicited to give their best input.

By contrast, when truth-telling is *not* a company value, then people start distorting information rather than reporting it openly. Members of a truth-avoidant company are tacitly taught to contend with mere symptoms, not root causes of problems. Whenever that happens, far too many people cave in to the pressure to conform to the perceived company norms. Over time, members of the company become more agreeable than honest.

So if a leader wants team members to give their very best input, they have to be invited to communicate authentically with each other. As long as members feel obligated to conform to some cookie-cutter image of whatever they believe the company wants, they'll continue to hold back, and the company will lose out as a result.

We can think of it like this—Strategists want the company to be *authentic*. Strategists want the people to be *free* in the sense of being unburdened by hidden problems that aren't addressed.

STRATEGISTS (Light)		
Freedom		
Authentic Community		

Now for the second category. Here I would write *Humanitarians* at the top of the second column.

Unlike the Strategists, the Humanitarians make their primary contribution by bringing *compassion* into the company. Humanitarians are the "people" people. They want the company to be a *comfortable* place to work. To put it metaphorically, the Humanitarians worry about the *temperature* in the company. They want the ethos either to feel warm and comfortable, or cool and refreshing. They can't stand it when the organizational climate becomes too heated or too chilled.

A company that fails to choose goodness as a core value ends up reducing people to mere units. People are then treated, not as human beings who are there to serve cooperatively as a team, but rather as machines who are there to make things happen impersonally as units of production. When a company forgets to take care of its own people, its life span inevitably is shortened. Over time, members of the company lose their creativity, and sometimes they also lose their drive.

So if a leader wants the team to give a unified best effort, then people must be nurtured along the way. For as long as a company's members feel exploited, they will not be able to improve continually, and the company will suffer as a result.

STRATEGISTS (Light)	HUMANITARIANS (Temp)
Freedom	*Compassion*
Authentic Community	*Comfortable Community*

Now let's take a look at the Diplomats. Imagine the word *Diplomats* at the top of the third column. The Diplomats are interested in bringing a sense of *peace* into the company. They seek an internal sense of peace from department to department and an external sense of peace between the company and the public. To put it metaphorically, the Diplomats value color. What I mean by *color* goes back to the idea of the Beautiful. The Diplomats beautify the company because they want it to be impressive; they want it to project a positive image and be valued by outsiders. Whereas Strategists want the company to *be* good, and Humanitarians want the company to *feel* good, Diplomats want the company to *look* good.

When diplomacy is devalued, all kinds of political problems can ensue—problems with city officials, problems with the federal government, problems with neighboring organizations, and the like. It doesn't take long for conflicting interests to arise both inside and outside an organization. Hence, an organization will be handicapped, even possibly shut down, if these conflicting interests are not arbitrated.

So if a leader wants team members to be skilled at handling conflict, then people need to practice being tactful and adroit. They need to exercise diplomacy, not only with the public, but with each other. Unless relational tensions are defused, an organization will suffer unnecessarily from internal discord, a loss of public confidence, or both.

STRATEGISTS (Light)	HUMANITARIANS (Temp)	DIPLOMATS (Color)
Freedom	Compassion	*Peace*
Authentic Community	Comfortable Community	*Impressive Community*
Be Good	*Feel Good*	*Look Good*

To clarify, the Humanitarians care about the ethos; the Diplomats care about appearances. If we fail to see this distinction, we might become confused and think the Diplomats' concern for peace is identical to the Humanitarians' concern for a comfortable ethos. So let me here insert an important point. The Diplomats are interested in bringing a *sense* of peace into the company. They see, better than Strategists and Humanitarians, that people need to be made aware of a company's strengths. To Diplomats, perceptions are critical, even on a personal level.

Consider this illustration. Almost thirty years ago, as a young teenager on a family vacation, I befriended an older woman who spent her afternoons sunbathing at the hotel swimming pool. She was middle-aged and white-skinned. After two or three days, I suddenly saw something that earlier had completely escaped my notice: The woman's eyes were not the same color. Presented with this marvel, I blurted out in fascination, "Oh my goodness! You have one very green eye and one very brown eye!" Unfortunately, the woman felt offended. She was markedly disappointed that her camouflage had failed to do its job.

To this day, I am still amazed at what I never did notice on my own—the woman wore two utterly dissimilar sets of makeup on each eye. When she pointed that out to me, I was doubly fascinated because the colors of her makeup on her left eye were so different from the colors on her right eye.

Here's how that relates to the People Model. The woman applied color to camouflage her mismatched eyes. By analogy, that's what Diplomats do. A Diplomat would argue that it's virtuous to impose a sense of harmony and order to a face—or likewise to a marketing campaign. Diplomats are gifted with an inborn sense of proportion. They understand what it takes to make something seem attractive.

Kathy
Myer

It's interesting to note that beauty is itself a matter of proportions, a combination of math and art. Denzel Washington, for example, is said to have a perfect face because his features are symmetrical. His eyebrows match, his cheeks are mirror images of one another, the left side of his jawbone perfectly corresponds to the right. If all you did was measure his face, you'd know why he's so handsome. None of his physical features are crooked or inconsistent or lopsided.

So you see, the idea of beauty also pertains to harmony and order. Harmony and order are relevant to ten thousand other things in the world of business: landscaping, zoning laws, arranging office furniture, dressing for success, investing in good signage, managing collaborative relationships, and dealing with the media.

One last example: A friend of mine is building an auditorium that seats four thousand people. What makes this auditorium so special is that the seats are color coded. The covers on the chairs are patterned in such a way that the room does not feel empty, even if no more than a hundred people are clustered in the front center section.

By way of comparison, while the Diplomats provide a sense of harmony and order, Strategists bring *clarity* and *accountability* to the table. There's nothing like clarity to get a Strategist pumped up, except a money-back guarantee that genuine accountability will follow.

As for the Humanitarians, they keep themselves busy facilitating other people's growth and success. They're the helpers, the leadership developers. They'll walk an extra mile in support of their supervisor and stay late to help a colleague in need. They mentor and give feedback. They open doors of opportunity, even when future up-and-coming leaders are too green to be considered up and coming. In short, the Humanitarians *support people*.

When it comes to their company, all three types care about

the organization as a whole. They do so, however, in dissimilar ways. The Strategists, for instance, focus on *integrity*. They want square pegs in square holes. For them, integrity points back to the idea of truth setting everybody free. If square pegs will come to terms with their squareness, then they can find their fit in square holes.

Diplomats and Humanitarians care about integrity too, but not for the sake of organizational purity. When Strategists talk about integrity, they orient the concept around truth. By contrast, when the Humanitarians talk about integrity, actually they're referring to *togetherness*. Etymologically, the word *integrity* is related to the word *integer*. An integer is a whole number as opposed to a fraction. The Humanitarians value wholeness. They strive for togetherness as if people in the company were a family. For Diplomats, integrity is more about *unity*. See the interconnections? *Unity, harmony, order, peace, oneness.* Diplomats can visualize oneness between a large variety of groups.

STRATEGISTS (Light)	HUMANITARIANS (Temp)	DIPLOMATS (Color)
Freedom	Compassion	Peace
Authentic Community	Comfortable Community	Impressive Community
Be Good	Feel Good	Look Good
Clarity, Accountability	*Develop, Support People*	*Sense of Harmony and Order*
Integrity	*Togetherness*	*Unity*

Now let's consider the ever-important distinction in the way the three groups handle conflict. With Strategists, you can pretty well count on hearing a *straightforward message* from them. If they're ticked, they tell you. And they expect you to do the same. It's unnecessary when talking to Strategists to beat around the bush for twenty minutes before finally getting around to the point. Just say it. Just tell them what the conflict is about. Trust them enough to give them a straightforward message. They want to know it because they ground their security in the truth.

With Humanitarians, conflict resolution is all about having a *wise approach*. To be effective with them, you've got to be gentle and concentrate on *how* things ought to be said. Humanitarians, for instance, intuitively will tend to affirm the person before addressing the conflict. At other times, they may tell a story or lead the person through an experience that prepares them to accept what the Humanitarian wants them to hear.

With Diplomats, the matter is slightly different. For them, dealing with conflict is synonymous with *wise timing*—searching for the right moment in which to speak. Diplomats are sensitive to the ambience in the room, the vibes between persons, and the sequencing of when each thing is said. For Diplomats the goal is to find that special *when* that promises to reestablish peace.

In summary, we could say that the Strategists are *confrontational*, the Humanitarians are *forbearing*, and the Diplomats are *nonconfrontational*.

Let's pause here long enough to talk about the difference between the idea of forbearance and the idea of being nonconfrontational. To forbear is to notice the problem and choose to endure it. In other words, to be forbearing is to endure another person's faults for the sake of being supportive of that person. To be nonconfrontational, however, is to overlook a person's faults for the sake of fostering unity in the company.

To better understand the People Model, it's helpful to consider some well-known leaders who seem to embody each type. Bear in mind, however, that a person's primary type may be dependent upon the given situation. Yet in spite of these fluctuations, most people tend to lean toward one of the three.

When I think of all the qualities of the Strategists, leaders such as William Buckley, Woodrow Wilson, Winston Churchill, and Condoleezza Rice come to mind. I imagine that Lee Iacocca fits best in this category too. Strategists tend to be *corrective*. It bothers them when things are out of whack. Strategists like solutions and results, and since they tend to be *discerning* and *analytical*, they can usually put their finger on the problem.

By contrast, Humanitarians tend to be *patient* and *kind*. They're usually good stabilizers, *loyal* to the company in general, and *loyal* to the people they work with. A few might include Nelson Mandela, Eleanor Roosevelt, Jimmy Carter, Herbert Hoover, and Andrew Carnegie.

Diplomats, by distinction, often have *charisma*. Usually they imbue a certain charm. They have an *artful demeanor*—which fits with their propensity to create a sense of harmony and order. Think of Ronald Reagan and Martin Luther King Jr. They also have *finesse*; Diplomats use their silver tongues to get their way. They can be *polished* like Bill Clinton or *refined* like Oprah Winfrey. Or they have an aura of credibility like Billy Graham.

All of the qualities named so far rest above the line. In the next chapter, we'll focus on the dark side of each category. But before you turn the page, I encourage you to study the chart.

Denise Amy   *Tammi Beth*

Debbie
Danice

STRATEGISTS (Light)	HUMANITARIANS (Temp)	DIPLOMATS (Color)
Freedom	Compassion	Peace
Authentic Community	Comfortable Community	Impressive Community
Be Good	Feel Good	Look Good
Clarity, Accountability	Develop, Support People	Sense of Harmony and Order
Integrity	Togetherness	Unity
Straightforward Message	*Wise Approach*	*Wise Timing*
Confrontational	*Forbearing*	*Nonconfrontational*
Discerning, Analytical	*Patient, Kind*	*Finesse, Artful Demeanor*
Corrective	*Loyal*	*Polished, Refined*

THREE BASIC SETS
OF WEAKNESSES

There are two parts to the People Model chart: the upper story and the lower story. The upstairs and the downstairs. The two parts are divided by a thick straight line. That horizontal line demarcates the border between above-the-line leadership and below-the-line leadership. The qualities above the line are assets to the company whereas the qualities below, as you will soon see, are liabilities.

When the Strategists drop below the line, immediately they become *self-righteous*. They assign themselves too much credit for being insightful and authentic. The Humanitarians, by contrast, become *self-serving*. Instinctively they serve themselves by making themselves feel comfortable. The Diplomats, however, reflexively become *self-absorbed*. They fall into the trap of narcissism.

When the root of each vice begins to bud, things in all three columns get worse. For example, the self-righteousness of the Strategists causes them to be *harsh* and *critical*. The Humanitarians become compromising *people pleasers*, and the Diplomats get stuck in *image management*.

STRATEGISTS (Light)	HUMANITARIANS (Temp)	DIPLOMATS (Color)
Freedom	Compassion	Peace
Authentic Community	Comfortable Community	Impressive Community
Be Good	Feel Good	Look Good
Clarity, Accountability	Develop, Support People	Sense of Harmony and Order
Integrity	Togetherness	Unity
Straightforward Message	Wise Approach	Wise Timing
Confrontational	Forbearing	Nonconfrontational
Discerning, Analytical	Patient, Kind	Finesse, Artful Demeanor
Corrective	Loyal	Polished, Refined
Self-Righteous	*Self-Serving*	*Self-Absorbed*
Criticism, Harshness	*People Pleasing*	*Image Management*

When the Strategists descend more deeply into the basement, they flat out become *self-righteously judgmental*. What we're talking about here is a certain type of judgment. It's necessary for people to exercise judgment in general. Most of us desire to have good judgment. We judge to see if our shoes fit before we buy them. We judge which banana to eat. We judge whom to trust. We judge how situations ought to be handled.

But self-righteous judgment—that's something altogether different. Self-righteous judgment is immoral and destructive and wrong. To judge self-righteously is to be arrogant. It's to evaluate on the basis of a prior assumption that says, "I'm the normative standard of morality. My superiority is a given."

I'm always amused when Humanitarians and Diplomats, in response to hearing the vices of the Strategists, respond by feeling glad that those things don't describe *them*. Their gladness, of course, is reflective of their own self-righteous judgment. I mention this because it provides a good example of how everyone is a mix of all three types. (Many people tell me that they know they're all three types because they see themselves *downstairs* in all three columns!) Unfortunately it's easy for anyone to be pulled below the line.

Another aspect of the Strategists' lower story is the tendency to be *presumptuous*. Presumption becomes destructive when it causes people to jump to false conclusions. To presume is to fill in the gaps with your own self-righteous judgment rather than waiting to let the truth unfold. Presumption can take the form of interrupting other people, disrespectfully finishing what you think they're going to say. Or it can do something worse—it can lead to prejudice. Prejudice refers to prejudgment—insidious prejudgment. To be prejudiced is to judge unfairly on the basis of a false presumption. In addition, Strategists are notorious for being *impatient*. They don't want to wait. They don't want to learn about something that they think they already know.

Another element in the downstairs of the Strategists' column is the propensity to *slander*. Slander is the verbal expression of self-righteous judgment. It's important to note the difference between slander and gossip. To gossip is to spread rumors. To slander is to tear someone down, to say things in a blunt or exaggerated way for the purpose of deriding someone's character.

By comparison, when the character of the Humanitarians degenerates, they *enable* other people's dark sides. They become the rescuers: the wives of alcoholics, the knights in shining armor who facilitate the distress of fretful damsels. Below-the-line Humanitarians accommodate and act complicitly in all kinds of company garbage. They enable other people because they're scared of other people. That's what sucks them down into their people-pleasing problem in the first place.

Whereas the Strategists are bold to blurt out anything, no matter how harsh or arrogant it sounds, the Humanitarians tend to be more tentative. The Humanitarians would sooner gossip than slander. What feeds their curiosity about other people's business is the guilt that they feel about themselves. It relieves the Humanitarians' fears and alleviates their guilt to hear the low-down dirty scoop on someone else. But the irony is that while the Humanitarians try to please people, they also have it in them to gossip in the shadows about the very people they are trying to make happy.

As a result of their enablement, the Humanitarians are liable to set themselves up to suffer as self-appointed martyrs. When slumped below the line, they thanklessly slave for the sake of other people while secretly feeling sorry for themselves. Even if you try to persuade them to take a break, they'll refuse to be relieved lest they forfeit their heroic magnanimity.

Why is that? What triggers the downstairs Humanitarians to acquire a *martyr complex*? Again, their sense of guilt. Humanitarians are overly loyal because they feel guilty *not* being overly loyal. It's their guilt that propels them to feel as if they have to overwork. Their guilt becomes the fuel that propels them to labor tirelessly, even when they need to go home and rest. As a matter of fact, that explains why the Humanitarians can sometimes feel resentful. Over time, if they're taken advantage of, they begin to resent the very people whom they're trying to please. They get mad because they really don't want to overwork. And yet they refuse to set firm boundaries by which to protect themselves.

Not surprisingly, the Humanitarians have a knack for laying guilt trips on other people. They dish out guilt by insisting that everyone else exhibit the same loyalty that they do—even when their loyalty is excessive. This, too, is tied to their people pleasing. In a below-the-line Humanitarian culture, often the cardinal sin becomes "disloyalty."

Now think about the Diplomats. The Diplomats have a different set of vices. When the Diplomats drop below the line, their tendency toward image management degenerates into *spin*. At their worst, Diplomats start spinning so much that they *distort* the truth, and even redefine the truth altogether. À la Clinton's famous statement during the Monica Lewinsky scandal: "It depends on what the meaning of the word *is* is."

Here's my observation. When Diplomats start distorting, doctoring up the truth, and trying to treat reality as if it were putty, it's hard to pin them down, especially when they rally a group of supporters whom I like to call the "spin club." The spin club refers to the cluster of people who are gulled into the spin. (Just in case you're wondering, even Strategists are susceptible to being swirled into the spin because the Strategist might presume that the Diplomat is telling the truth.)

The situation can conceivably get worse. If a Diplomat, for instance, is hiding information or lying outright—and starts getting caught—the spin will start to thicken. Diplomats have the skills to convince a number of people that they're innocent when they're guilty. They'll use their calmness, their refinement, their charisma, their artful demeanor—whatever it is they've got. They'll use all of it to protect the all-important image that they're managing.

Renegade Diplomats have two additional propensities that

I believe describe them at their worst. First, they *intimidate* people politically. That is, they psych people out by bluffing. They pretend to have more collateral than they actually have. They try to scare the socks off people. They take advantage of everyone who is worried about the political ramifications that may possibly arise with holding a guilty Diplomat accountable.

Second, what a Diplomat will do when caught like a rat in a corner is flip the situation into reverse. Let me put it this way. When Diplomats feel threatened, they will *not* assume the role of a martyr—as a Humanitarian would do. Neither will they act as a self-appointed judge—which is what a Strategist would do. Rather, a Diplomat will take on the role of a *victim.*

Here again they will appeal to the spin club—for sympathy, asylum, public protests, or whatever they might need. All for the sake of maintaining their persona.

The Diplomat in all of us can be difficult to hold accountable. I have long held the belief that every person on the planet can at times be an Oscar-winning liar, especially when caught in a bind.

As you look at the chart on page 25, notice that the items preceded by dashes stem from the behaviors written above them.

There's more to the model. What I have presented thus far is just the beginning. Once you read the story in part 2, you'll see the model's implications. I have chosen to tell a story because a narrative best explains how the model plays out in real life.

I might add here that the story is fictitious, yet its plot is actually thousands of years old. It's a classic ancient story that repeats itself in every generation from time to time. Thus the story could be set almost anywhere—in a business, a nonprofit, some kind of government structure, or even in a volunteer club.

So on the one hand, the story is a parable. None of the char-

	STRATEGISTS (Light)	HUMANITARIANS (Temp)	DIPLOMATS (Color)
	Freedom	Compassion	Peace
	Authentic Community	Comfortable Community	Impressive Community
	Be Good	Feel Good	Look Good
	Clarity, Accountability	Develop, Support People	Sense of Harmony and Order
	Integrity	Togetherness	Unity
	Straightforward Message	Wise Approach	Wise Timing
	Confrontational	Forbearing	Nonconfrontational
	Discerning, Analytical	Patient, Kind	Finesse, Artful Demeanor
	Corrective	Loyal	Polished, Refined
	Self-Righteous	Self-Serving	Self-Absorbed
	Criticism, Harshness	People Pleasing	Image Management
BEHAVIOR:	Self-Righteous Judgment	Enablement	Spin (Spin Club)
	—Slander	—Gossip	—Distorts, Redefines Truth
	—Presumption	—Guilt Trips	—Political Intimidation
	—Impatience	—Martyr Complex	—Victim of Circumstances

acters are real people. On the other hand, all of the characters represent people that you know. Since the story serves the purpose of illuminating the People Model further, I decided to make the main character (John Mark) its inventor. That way he becomes the voice to introduce the model to everyone else in the narrative.

To prepare you for the dialogue, allow me to introduce you to the five lead characters in the story:

John Mark, *the vice president of sales*
Cynthia, *John Mark's wife*
Max, *the CEO and president of the company*

Nathan, *the executive vice president*
Lisa, *John Mark's mentoree who works in public relations and also as a consultant to Max, the president*

The setting is Philadelphia at the headquarters of a fictitious service company called WeServTech (WST). But the story could happen anywhere because the crux of it has to do with leadership and character development. This is a story about leadership and people rather than any particular industry.

So now meet John Mark and his wife, Cynthia, as they debrief after work in the privacy of their home, and be careful along the way to absorb as many details as you can, because the answer to many questions that leaders often face are embedded in the story's conversations.

PART TWO

THE NARRATIVE

CHAPTER 4

THE BIRTH OF
THE PEOPLE MODEL

"Nathan just doesn't get it," John Mark said to his wife.

Cynthia looked at him sympathetically as she rubbed her weary feet.

"I have tried and tried to talk to him," he said. "I tried again today, but as usual, I couldn't get anywhere with him."

She sighed. "You sound disappointed again."

"I *am* disappointed again. What will it take to get this supervisor of mine to understand that I'm on his team—that I'm actually trying to help him?"

"Are you feeling unappreciated?" She put her nursing shoes in the closet.

"No. I feel frustrated," he answered. "I'm bothered because I can't tap into his wavelength. I don't know how to get through to him. It's almost as if he can't hear me."

"What do you want him to hear?"

"I want him to hear that he's sabotaging himself," said John Mark.

"Is he willing to hear that?" said Cynthia, motioning to her husband to follow her downstairs into the kitchen.

"Maybe not, but he needs to."

"Why do you have to be the one to tell him?" she asked.

"Because I see the problem," said John Mark. "When you're watching someone play with fire, you speak up and warn them. That's the only right thing to do."

"What kind of fire is he playing with?" asked Cynthia.

"He's ignoring reality."

"What do you mean? From what you've told me in the past, Nathan seems to be aware of a number of things."

"Like what?"

"Like the customers. Nathan knows all the major customers by name. He's really very good at meeting people."

John Mark countered, "I agree that Nathan is adept at public relations. My point is that while Nathan makes an effort to learn our customers' names, he doesn't really care about them as people. His big concern in business is to make a big name for himself."

"And that's frustrating to you," she said.

"That's what drives me crazy," he confirmed. "Nathan can't appreciate good advice. Take today, for instance. I couldn't have made myself any plainer. During our weekly team meeting, he told us he was planning a few changes to make us more competitive. But you know what he wanted to do? His idea was to violate our marketing schedule! He wanted us to start promising services to potential new clients that we aren't even capable of providing yet. We have strict company guidelines in place to prevent such misrepresentations."

John Mark pulled a bar stool away from the counter and sat down.

"What did you say to him?" asked Cynthia.

"I told him there'd be a boomerang effect if he fudges too much on the rules. That it will come back to haunt him if he makes misleading claims to our customers."

"Why would Nathan want to break the rules?"

"Because he doesn't believe in following rules," said John Mark. "He likes for others to follow rules, so that he will have an advantage when he breaks them."

Cynthia looked at her husband skeptically.

"Believe me, this is par for the course for him. From Nathan's perspective, the sky is the limit because no rules have the power to hold him back."

"So how did he respond when you told him that the company can't implement his plan?"

"He got this silly grin on his face. I don't know how to describe it. It wasn't sinister, but it wasn't innocent either. I guess that you could say it was peculiar. His mouth gaped a little and that peculiar grin set in, and then he said flippantly, 'Why?'"

Cynthia replied, "He wanted to know why it's wrong to break company rules?"

John Mark answered, "No, he was telling me that since it doesn't seem wrong to *him*, then the company shouldn't think it's wrong either."

"Are you sure that's what he meant?"

John Mark replied, "It adds up with everything else. Think about it. Nathan lives in his own world. He can't see the difference between his own imagination and reality. In fact, I believe that Nathan sees the company as an extension of himself. And let's face it, Cynthia, Nathan has unusual self-regard."

"You couldn't get through to him today at all?"

"Not on the main point that I was trying to make."

Cynthia sighed. "Well, I can see why you feel upset."

"It's annoying," said John Mark. "I mean, I'm trying to help the guy. But he elevates himself so far above the rest of us that he simply can't conceive of needing to make changes in himself."

"Does anyone else see a problem in Nathan?" Cynthia asked.

"Almost all of us who work for him see the problem in spades. We talk about it openly. Unfortunately, I'm the only one who has confronted Nathan personally. The others are too afraid. Nathan can be so intimidating. He drops these little hints about not wanting anyone to be fired."

"Yeah, that scares me too. I hope you don't lose your job," said Cynthia.

"I'm not worried about that," said John Mark. "I'm worried about the mess that is likely to ensue. My fear is that Nathan will stay in the company just long enough to create a disaster, and then he'll move to another company. I'll be left there, along with a few others, to sort through all the debris."

"How long has Nathan been a part of the company? About six or seven years?"

"Yes, and as far as I can tell, he still has no interest in studying reports, or holding anyone accountable, or paying due respect to the budget."

"But he's the executive vice president. How can he get away with that?"

"Because Nathan was promoted from the PR department by none other than Max," said John Mark. "He's 'Max's boy,' and Max is the CEO."

"Max must see something valuable in Nathan."

"There's no doubt that Nathan is talented. You've seen him," said John Mark. "He's long-winded at times, but he can make an excellent first impression."

"Yeah," said Cynthia. "I remember how excited you were when Nathan first got the job. You said he was going to be a great role model."

"That's another disappointment," said John Mark. "While it's true that I can learn something from Nathan's way of uniting people, mostly I have learned from him what not to do. How not to lead."

"What makes Max think that Nathan holds promise for the company?"

"Max looks at Nathan, not the facts."

"What do you mean?" asked Cynthia.

"I mean just what I said. Max looks at Nathan, and Nathan looks good. His hygiene is immaculate, and his level of self-confidence is exceptional."

Cynthia replied, "I must admit that Nathan is rather impressive when he speaks. Didn't you tell me that WeServTech was awarded exclusive servicing rights by the state's university system after Nathan made a pitch at their board meeting?"

"Yes . . . after the rest of us had been meeting and planning our approach for months on end."

Cynthia raised an eyebrow as she looked at John Mark.

"Look, I'll admit Nathan's got charisma. He's convincing to those who watch him," said John Mark. "He looks good and sounds good as long as you don't listen to what he says."

"How can he sound good to people who aren't listening?" asked Cynthia.

John Mark tried to explain. "It's the tone of Nathan's voice that sounds good. That is, his voice sounds good if you listen to nothing more than its sound. When you listen to the content of what he says, you notice right away it's a bunch of hollow words."

"So what do you think is going to happen?" asked Cynthia. She opened the door of the oven to check if their dinner was hot.

"I don't know because I don't see the numbers firsthand," said John Mark, bouncing his heels. "But I do see Nathan's habits, and I'm telling you—the numbers have to be down. You can't spend money the way that Nathan does without compromising the final results."

"Well, if things go awry, it won't be your fault," said Cynthia.

"What do you mean 'if'?" said John Mark. "Things have already gone awry. If you ask me, we're taking the scenic route on a quiet collision course headed steadily and directly for a crash. I wish someone could communicate that to Max."

"I'm surprised that you haven't tipped him off yourself." Cynthia thought for a second. "Have you talked to Max already?"

John Mark nodded.

"What did you say to him?" she asked.

"I told him that I don't trust Nathan."

"What did Max say in return?"

"He said that Nathan is on a learning curve, and he asked me to help him out as much as I can."

"When did that happen?" asked Cynthia.

"About three months ago."

"You've been trying to help Nathan for three months?" she said incredulously. "No wonder you feel frustrated."

John Mark agreed. "I don't like having a boss who breaks the rules."

"Well, if it's any consolation, Max has always been good to you. I guess the best we can do is trust his judgment."

John Mark couldn't stand to hear this, so he got up and left the room. Soon Cynthia heard the sound of a newspaper being whipped open a bit too loudly and abruptly.

Cynthia peered into the living room. "Honestly, I was trying to console you. Can I get you something to drink?"

"It doesn't console me to know that you trust Max's judgment more than you trust mine."

"What?" said Cynthia. "You don't think I trust your judgment? What gave you that idea?"

"I told you my assessment of the situation at work, and your response, in effect, was to say that I'm probably wrong."

"I didn't say that you were wrong."

"Think about what you *did* say," John Mark replied.

Cynthia recounted the conversation. "I asked you about Max, and then I said that the best thing we can do is trust . . ."

It dawned on her now what she had said.

Trying to win back her husband, Cynthia said, "First your frustration was with Nathan, then it was with Max, and now it is with me." She paused for a second. "My intention was to make you feel better."

John Mark loosened up. "I know. I'm sorry for losing my cool."

———

The next morning at the office, as John Mark was checking his e-mails, he heard his secretary greeting Nathan.

"Good morning," she said.

John Mark looked up from his computer. There was Nathan smiling at the secretary as if she were taking his photo. His suit was immaculate and his shirt pocket monogrammed. Indeed, every article of his clothing was perfect. Nevertheless, he paused to straighten his jacket before tapping his manicured fingers on John Mark's open door.

"How are you?" asked Nathan, extending his hand.

"Good," said John Mark, standing up. The two of them shook hands.

"What's up?" said John Mark.

"There's a special opportunity," said Nathan. "It's very prestigious, in fact. We need someone, someone trustworthy like you, John Mark, to take charge of a new initiative. The plan is to set up a formal system of leadership development within the company. Max loves the idea, and he's excited that I've selected you as the leader to jump-start it."

"You're asking me to do this on top of my regular job?"

"Not exactly," said Nathan. "We would divvy up a portion of your current responsibilities, so that a third of your time would be freed up during this quarter, and then half of your time from then on."

"Am I failing to measure up in my current role?"

"Just the opposite," said Nathan. "You've made a unique contribution as the vice president of sales. Your team seems to love you, and you've brought in some solid new customers. There's a lot to be said about your success. But I think I have identified the next step for you, John Mark. Granted, we'll have to change a few things here at headquarters in order to accommodate this important transition, but it's time to shuffle the cards."

John Mark responded, "I have more responsibility in my current role full-time than I would have in starting a new program for fledgling leaders."

"There are perks to this opportunity," said Nathan. "To begin with, you'd have a nice office on the other side of the complex looking out at the company pond. The work pressure on you would be lightened, so that you would have plenty of time to innovate new ideas for upcoming leaders. There are countless benefits to taking this job. Perhaps the most significant one is that you would be given the chance to demonstrate your exceptional abilities in a context that will highlight your achievements."

Nathan placed a paternal hand upon John Mark's shoulder and concluded with the remark, "John Mark, one of your distinctions as a third-tier leader is that you have expertise in both operations and sales. You're a treasured hybrid. That's why you're the man for the job."

"Would I still be the vice president of sales?" John Mark lowered himself into his chair.

"Yes, for at least six months, you would. But the ultimate goal, of course, would be for you to transition into the other role full-time."

"Who do you have in mind to replace me?"

"I haven't gotten that far," said Nathan.

He seated himself, mirroring John Mark's posture.

"I want to honor you in this process. This is your moment, John Mark, and I'm not willing to detract from the celebration of your stepping out in fortitude to seize it. You have that pioneering spirit, and Max and I want to take advantage of it."

John Mark responded, "Nathan, if you start rearranging the organizational chart without processing your ideas with anyone else on the team, you're setting yourself up for a windstorm. When you move people around, you're asking whole families to make adjustments. What's your rationale for this plan?"

Nathan looked smugly at John Mark as if to say he felt no obligation to answer the question.

John Mark broke the silence. "I don't believe you *have* a rationale. If I can speak candidly with you, Nathan, my observation is that you routinely operate without plans, rationale, or any clear processes by which to communicate your ideas to the team."

John Mark braced himself to hear a long defense from his wordy supervisor. But to John Mark's surprise, Nathan responded as if he were accepting an award. He leaned against the file cabinet and answered nondefensively.

"That's probably fair for you to say," said Nathan in a reflective, self-congratulatory tone. "I'm more fortunate than most. Since I run on intuition, I don't have to grapple with all the data that tends to bog down other leaders. Instead I have the advantage of being endowed with a sixth sense; you know, a natural feel for things. I get hunches of what needs to be done, and then I wait until the time seems right to do it."

Cutting the conversation short, Nathan stood up and disingenuously expressed a large measure of appreciation for John Mark's willingness to volunteer for the new role. Then he bid John Mark good-bye and walked away.

John Mark sat motionless until the moment that Nathan's foot stepped out the door. Then he swiveled his chair around and composed an urgent e-mail to Max:

Dear Max,
I'm writing to explain to you in no uncertain terms that I declined Nathan's offer this morning to lead the start-up for leadership development within the company. I am fully committed to my role as vice president of sales.
John Mark

Later that day, John Mark received an e-mail back from Max.

John Mark,

It was my understanding that you had expressed to Nathan an interest in the leadership development initiative. If you prefer not to lead the charge, I will honor your request. Thanks for being such a hard worker.

Max

———

That evening before bed John Mark recounted the episode to his wife.

"Can you believe that Nathan ended the meeting by thanking me for *volunteering* for the job? I'm telling you, Cynthia, he's deluded."

"I hope he doesn't try to get you fired," said Cynthia. "It scares me to think of what Nathan might do when he finds out from Max that you declined his special offer. It's probably going to embarrass him, John Mark."

"No need to worry," said John Mark. "Nathan will spin his way out of it. He'll probably tell Max that I misunderstood our conversation."

Cynthia shook her head in disbelief.

John Mark added, "I won't lose my job. I may lose my sanity, but I am quite securely positioned. I now have it in writing that Max has agreed to honor my request."

"Is that why you e-mailed Max? To get something back from him in writing?"

"I'm not stupid," said John Mark.

"I know you do things for a reason," said Cynthia. "But I missed it on this one. I thought you wrote him because you didn't want to duke it out with Nathan."

"You're projecting," said John Mark. "You're the one who's always avoiding conflict."

"Well, I must say that was very clever," said Cynthia.

John Mark smiled. It felt nice to be admired by his wife. Ever since Nathan had become his supervisor, John Mark had felt less and less admired in the workplace. Though his colleagues still looked up to him, he didn't feel their appreciation quite as much. He had become the conscience of the company, and the others made him pay a price for that.

It took him hours to fall asleep that night. His mind kept bombarding him with questions. *Why am I becoming so critical? And why do I feel so alone? Why can't I just do what Cynthia says and trust Max?*

He tossed and turned in bed, but still his thoughts kept racing. *Why can't Nathan hear me? And why won't the others speak up? Why does Max believe in Nathan? Why are all these problems so obvious to me? And why do I feel stirred to sort them out?*

Though eventually John Mark fell asleep, at a subconscious level, he remained in a state of consternation. Over the next several weeks, he effectively assimilated almost every observation that he had. He did this apart from any conscious realization that he was innovating a revelatory idea. Soon he would discover that a fresh new way of thinking, a fruitful paradigm, had outcropped on the landscape of his mind.

CHAPTER 5

A COMPLEX
SITUATION

The next week John Mark was summoned into Nathan Gorman's office. He was not given advance notice. Nor did Nathan contact him directly—as usual, he relied on his own secretary for that.

"John Mark?" she had said in a kind, embarrassed tone. "Nathan would like to see you right away. He said to make sure there's no delay."

When John Mark arrived, he noticed that Nathan greeted him as if he were a lifelong family friend.

"John Mark, so good to see you," said Nathan.

John Mark immediately sensed a big elephant in the room, but he couldn't yet discern what Nathan was up to.

"John Mark, we need you," said Nathan in his most solemn voice. "Our cash flow is tight, so we need you to saddle back into the sales force and ride into the frontier and do your thing. You're the best salesperson in the company. There are others who can lead, but virtually no one who can sell as well as you. As the executive vice president, I feel that it's my duty to reposition you at this time for the sake of the budget."

"My budget isn't tight," said John Mark. "We're in the black on my side of the company."

"That's exactly why I've chosen you," said Nathan. "You're an awesome numbers guy. You can get the numbers to add up."

"The accountants are the numbers people," retorted John Mark.

"But you've got the golden touch to affect the bottom line," Nathan countered.

"Nathan, I'm not interested in leaving my post. We've already been through this."

"I know you're happy now," said Nathan. "But unfortunately, I'm not in a position to be able to accommodate your very reasonable request. Strategy calls for a repositioning at this time. It almost breaks my heart to have to do this, but it consoles me to know that you're likely to make more money in this new arrangement. You will be entitled to a nice fat bonus if you can meet the quota I have set for you."

"I knew it," said Cynthia on her cell phone. "I could feel it in my bones that Nathan was going to push you out of the inner circle."

"I didn't think he could get away with it," said John Mark, making sure that his office door was shut.

"Did you talk to Max yet?" Cynthia asked. She was driving to the hospital to work her afternoon shift.

"Yeah, he said that there's a personality clash between me and Nathan."

"A personality clash? He reduced it to that?"

"You know Max," said John Mark. "He doesn't have a malicious bone in his body. He told me that he's trying to give Nathan some space to lead. He doesn't want to micromanage him."

"You'll be traveling a lot again, won't you," Cynthia predicted. Her eyes flooded with tears. Now that their kids were in college, she found that it was lonely to be home without John Mark.

"The part that really irks me," he explained, "is that Nathan is trying to use me to fund his irresponsible spending habits. Cynthia, the *last* thing I want to do is rescue him."

"You're not planning to leave the company altogether, are you?" she asked. Cynthia loved her job and didn't want to think about relocating.

"I'm not ready to leave yet," said John Mark. "But I dread seeing what happens after Nathan wrecks the sales team."

"How can he live with himself?" said Cynthia.

"Because he'll tell himself that he's *building* a new team."

"This is sickening," Cynthia groaned.

"It's tragic," said John Mark.

"And Max is going to stand by and watch all this take place?"

"Max is swamped right now," said John Mark. "He doesn't have time to do both his job and Nathan's. Who knows what impression Max has been given at this point. Nathan could've told him anything."

"It's rare for you to be this suspicious," said Cynthia.

"I do *not* trust Nathan Gorman," said John Mark.

When the sales team found out that Nathan was demoting John Mark, they responded with predictable questions:

"You're moving John Mark out?"

"Is this decision finalized already?"

"Is there any particular reason why we weren't given any notice beforehand?"

"What specifically occasioned this big change?"

"Who's going to be our new leader?"

After Nathan told the group that the change was necessary for strategic planning, they said nothing more out loud.

The next day another colleague, Lisa, stopped by to see John Mark. He was in his office reviewing a sales report. Lisa and John Mark had been friends for almost seven years. He had been assigned to serve as Lisa's mentor back when she worked in sales during her first few years of service with the company.

John Mark had never seen anyone better at really listening to her customers and tailoring WeServTech's services to meet their needs. Within three years, marketing had recruited her to a management position where she continued to distinguish herself. A few years later, she had found another niche in public relations. Though the requirement of their meetings had long been fulfilled, John Mark and Lisa had agreed to meet informally upon occasion for mutual sharpening.

"Hey, John Mark," said Lisa. "I hear you're back in the field."

John Mark looked up. "Word gets around fast."

"Nathan told me he's never seen a more natural salesperson than you," Lisa added.

John Mark turned his gaze back to the sales report.

Lisa sighed. She moved closer to John Mark's desk and lowered her voice. "I'm sorry it worked out this way."

He lifted his eyes and said, "Thanks, Lisa. I just hope that Nathan doesn't get the opportunity to tear up other sections of the company."

———

About seven months later, Nathan finished his first year in his job as executive vice president. John Mark knew that it appeared that Nathan had managed fairly well, but he thought the outward signs were misleading. Yes, Nathan had networked internally enough to have established a strong rapport with the executive team. And, yes, he had established a greater sense of unity between the business side and service side of the company. But Nathan had dismissed John Mark's clear advice about honoring internal regulations. He had also blown the budget. Nevertheless, in his public remarks, Max had deemphasized the unexposed facts and stressed instead that, in partnership with himself, Nathan had garnered the confidence of the biggest potential customer in the company's history.

So at 4:58 p.m. on Friday afternoon when the office of the president sent a company-wide e-mail that said the number two person had "stepped down," almost everyone who saw it was shocked.

John Mark, for instance, had never been more stunned in his life. He sat like a zombie at his computer.

How can this be? Just last week Nathan was crowing like a rooster about his latest ideas for expanding the company's borders. Besides, who else would hire him? He doesn't have the skills to build a sales team or crunch numbers or do research. He's the worst supervisor I've ever seen. Surely no one from the outside is trying to take him.

While John Mark sat frozen in his office, the sales team and the secretaries started gossiping.

"It sounds rather scandalous to me," someone whispered.

"There's no way that Nathan 'stepped down,' unless they forced him."

"What do you think happened?"

"In this day and age, we'll never know. It's organizational suicide for the board to tell the problem to the stakeholders."

"What if there *was* no problem, except bad management from the top?"

"Wait a minute, folks. You guys are making it sound like he was fired."

"You don't know half the story; Nathan should've been ousted months ago."

"The rumor is that he doesn't even know what he did wrong."

"Of course he doesn't know what he did wrong. That makes perfect sense if you think about it. Nathan has no self-awareness."

"According to the people who know him best, he was thrown into a tailspin by the news."

"Oh yeah, then why is there a story circulating?"

"It's none of our business. We shouldn't be talking about this."

"Okay, from now on, let's vow never to discuss any company-wide announcements that are disseminated from the office of the president."

Over the weekend the flames of company gossip blazed into a roar. First, the news came out that Nathan, indeed, had *not* stepped down. Second, employees learned that Nathan had been placed in a lower-ranking job. Aside from that, the details of the story were unconfirmed. Needless to say, people in the company kept conjecturing.

"Why transfer Nathan to a lower position? Why not let him go and give him severance pay?"

"Why not put him back in public relations?"

"Something must have happened."

"In this litigious environment, it's hush-hush."

"That won't stop the phone from ringing this week."

"I heard he messed things up with a major customer."

"I heard that he secured a major customer."

"I heard there was an issue with the budget."

"I heard that he locked horns with the president."

"I talked to Nathan myself and saw the tears of betrayal in his eyes."

"Oh please, and you fell for that?"

"What did he say when you saw him?"

"He said they pulled the rug out from under him. A total stealth move on the company's part."

"Makes you wonder if the president felt threatened . . . or jealous."

When John Mark checked his e-mail on that Saturday, sure enough, he found an additional communiqué in his in-box. It said that Nathan was going to work in leadership development full-time. John Mark grabbed his cell phone to call Cynthia.

"You're never going to believe this," he said. "Take a wild guess where Nathan will be working from now on."

"On the sales team with you," she said.

"No. Nathan has been appointed to serve as the founding leader for a leadership development program housed within the company."

"I thought that was a part-time job," said Cynthia.

"Originally, it was. But obviously Max increased it to a full-time position so that Nathan would have a parachute."

"Why would Max want to do that?" she asked.

"I have no idea. Several different stories are circulating. The most credible one to me is that Max is afraid because Nathan has friends on the board."

"If Max is afraid, then why transition him at all?"

"Because Nathan finally pushed the envelope too far," said John Mark.

"What do you mean by that?" asked Cynthia.

"Nathan doesn't respect the company culture. He got away with it for a while, but now the chips are down—Nathan simply broke too many rules."

"How do you know for sure?"

"Because it all adds up," said John Mark.

"You think he's being punished?"

"Yes and no," said John Mark. "Yes, he's being demoted. Perhaps that could be counted as a punishment. But no, he isn't being punished; he's hardly even being held accountable."

"Is Max going to reinstate you into your old job?"

"I doubt it," said John Mark. "It's hard on people to reshuffle all the time. Max is fairly sensitive to that."

"Well, this certainly is a surprising turn of events," said Cynthia. "I'm sure you've talked to Lisa by now. She knows what it's like to work with Nathan."

"Yeah, but when Lisa worked with Nathan in public relations, he worked independently—he wasn't a supervisor, and he didn't have to manage a large budget."

Early on Monday morning Max called for a mandatory meeting with the twenty-two people most directly impacted by the prior week's leadership change. He brought the CFO along with him to do almost all of the talking. In so many words, the CFO said this: "Nathan Gorman continues to be an asset to this company, and that's why he's moving to this significant position in leadership development."

To that, Max graciously concluded, "I have known Nathan for a number of years, and I will always be grateful for him."

Subsequently, questions were both fielded and evaded by the CFO, who brought closure to the meeting by explaining to the group that Nathan's responsibilities would largely be transferred to the COO until further notice.

At a superficial level, the rumblings settled down pretty quickly. Yet under the veneer of "business as usual," people were politically divided. There were two groups: defenders of the president and defenders of Nathan Gorman. Those who sided with the president were those who argued that the company had been weakened by Nathan's poor performance. Those who sided with Nathan, however, thought he had been marginalized unfairly.

Three weeks later at a quarterly meeting, Nathan Gorman was commended explicitly by name in a formal speech delivered by none other than Max. Memorable word sets such as "sterling character" and "creative contribution" were enunciated proudly from the platform.

As soon as Max sat down, the smoldering embers of gossip were stoked back into flames once again.

"Did Max just say what I thought he said?"

"Shhh, Nathan's sitting over there."

"I thought the Nathan story had ended."

"Why is our president kissing up to a subordinate?"

"Maybe he's regretting his decision."

"Maybe he's afraid of a lawsuit."

"You think Nathan would sue the company?"

"Why in the world would Max put someone so volatile in charge of leadership development?"

Lisa sat next to John Mark. While John Mark was fidgety, Lisa sat calmly and still. Even so, John Mark suspected she was bothered inside, and he marveled at her ability not to show it. She was sitting with great poise and aplomb. Had he not known her well, John Mark never would have guessed that she was racked to hear the things that Max was saying. But since he knew her, he was convinced that Lisa was struggling to ignore the refrain of praises that flowed from the president's mouth. John Mark knew how important it was to Lisa to be able to trust the company's CEO.

Still, Lisa said nothing except small talk during the meeting. John Mark appreciated her sense of propriety, and he knew she had extended it on his behalf as well. In hindsight, he also realized it must have been tough at times for her to be formally mentored by him. In almost every interchange, he had offered her a load of constructive criticism. How many times had he reminded Lisa that correction holds the key to securing a competitive advantage!

"No clarity," he would say, "then no accountability. And with no accountability, the company won't achieve the right results."

He knew he could be intense. In his very first conversation with her he had vouched for "vulnerability" as the number one need between people in the company, touting it as the basis for building trust.

"Team members have to be vulnerable," he had said. "They have to build a habit of leveling with each other. If they don't, the company will eventually lose out. Mark my words: When people gloss over the truth, they stop trusting one another. So I'm telling you from the start, be honest. Dare to bring the truth out into the open."

The following afternoon Lisa met John Mark at a local coffeehouse.

"Interesting speech last night," said Lisa. John Mark took that as an invitation to give his take on the baffling situation in the company, especially with regard to the inconsistent messages from Max.

John Mark believed—though Lisa probably wouldn't have admitted it, even to herself—that she was a benevolent opportunist. Certainly she wanted WeServTech to live up to its reputation, but her higher priority was to guard her favored standing with the president. Lisa had a knack for positioning herself politically with the power at the top.

John Mark responded, "I thought Max had had it with Nathan, but I guess not."

"Nathan has a lot to contribute," said Lisa.

"A lot of problems to contribute," he retorted.

"You know I think it was wrong for Nathan to have moved you, don't you?" she asked.

"But overall, you're sympathetic with him."

"I know he has liabilities."

"And yet he's being asked to multiply himself! Can you imagine having more Nathans in the company, now that he's developing the new leaders?"

"I agree that Nathan would benefit from learning how to be a little better team player," she suggested.

"A little better?" said John Mark.

Lisa responded, "I know you have a hard time with him, John Mark, but Nathan has a good side. He's always nice to me."

"He's nice to you because you report directly to Max. Nathan isn't stupid, Lisa. He knows good and well whom he can and cannot mess with."

"What do you think Max was trying to say last night?" Lisa asked.

"Why ask me? You know Max better than I do."

"Yeah, but I'm unsure of his intentions. It may be that Max was attempting to strengthen the company's unity. He might have been trying to tell us that he and Nathan are still a team and that there isn't any need for people in the company to take sides."

"But you're not convinced," said John Mark.

"Let's just say that I'm wondering," said Lisa.

"Wondering what?" asked John Mark.

"Wondering if there's a little more to it than that."

"You mean you're wondering if the truth is being told?" asked John Mark.

"I don't know if I would put it that starkly," she said. "But yeah, I'm probably hinting at that."

"You know what I've decided?" said John Mark. "Some people can deal with truth better than others."

"What do you mean?"

"Some people listen for truth, and some people listen for emotions—they're more sensitive to feelings than to facts. Others hear the *sound* of things; they hear the attitudes and tones of people's voices."

"Facts versus feelings versus sounds," said Lisa. "That's intriguing."

John Mark added, "If you listen for people's feelings, you don't hear the same messages as when you're listening for the facts or to the sounds."

"What are you getting at?" asked Lisa.

"I'm saying that people *hear* differently because they *think* differently. The best way I can explain it is by introducing you to a model that I've been testing on myself for several months."

"A model?" Lisa said. "Is it something that you found in a book?"

"No, it's something I developed myself," he explained. "I know this sounds a little odd, but like a symphony, it just came to me. There it was one day—this music in my head—just waiting to be scored and performed."

"It popped into your head all at once?"

"Basically, yeah," said John Mark. He smiled at her and added, "I call it the People Model."

"Is it relevant to business?" Lisa asked.

"It's relevant to any group of people."

"Then it's relevant to us," she said. "Is that right?"

"Yes," said John Mark. "It contains the power to make sense of some of the craziness that companies experience every day."

CHAPTER 6

THREE TYPES OF
EXECUTIVE LEADERS

Over the next hour or so, John Mark presented the categories of the People Model to Lisa. As soon as he finished, Lisa said to him, "That's fascinating."

"Do you think people will buy into the categories?" asked John Mark.

"I do," said Lisa. "But I also wonder if people might question your notion of truth. I don't want to put you on the spot, but you're one of the few execs who even believe in objective truth, or that there is such a thing as capital 'T' *truth* out there waiting to be discovered and known."

"Do you know *why* I believe that truth is objective?" he asked.

"With all due respect, it might be because you're old-fashioned," said Lisa.

"What if I put it this way?" he retorted. "Everyone knows what truth is because everybody knows how to lie."

Lisa threw her head back and laughed. "Where do you come up with these one-liners? I've never heard anyone say that."

"I'm a Strategist," he bantered. "I can't help myself."

"I would concur with that," said Lisa. "You're a Strategist, Max is a Humanitarian, and I'm a Diplomat."

John Mark interjected, "And yet everyone is a mix of all three types."

Lisa congratulated him. "The People Model is great. Actually, I'd like to have a copy of it. But honestly, I wish that no one else would see it."

	STRATEGISTS (Light)	HUMANITARIANS (Temp)	DIPLOMATS (Color)
	Freedom	Compassion	Peace
	Authentic Community	Comfortable Community	Impressive Community
	Be Good	Feel Good	Look Good
	Clarity, Accountability	Develop, Support People	Sense of Harmony and Order
	Integrity	Togetherness	Unity
	Straightforward Message	Wise Approach	Wise Timing
	Confrontational	Forbearing	Nonconfrontational
	Discerning, Analytical	Patient, Kind	Finesse, Artful Demeanor
	Corrective	Loyal	Polished, Refined
	Self-Righteous	Self-Serving	Self-Absorbed
	Criticism, Harshness	People Pleasing	Image Management
BEHAVIOR:	Self-Righteous Judgment	Enablement	Spin (Spin Club)
	—Slander	—Gossip	—Distorts, Redefines Truth
	—Presumption	—Guilt Trips	—Political Intimidation
	—Impatience	—Martyr Complex	—Victim of Circumstances

John Mark burst out laughing. He correctly guessed that she wanted to keep the model all to herself because she didn't want anyone else to know her style.

"Let me see if I've got this straight," said John Mark. "You like the model, but you want to keep it to yourself. Now why, may I ask, could that be?"

"I want people to trust me," she announced. "If people peg me as a Diplomat, they might not trust me as much. I'd rather have people think that I'm a Strategist."

John Mark thought her comment was hilarious. "You mean, you esteem truth-telling enough to pretend to be a Strategist? You would *lie* for the sake of that cause? Wow, Lisa, I'm inspired by your noble convictions."

Lisa laughed.

"Let's get this straight," John Mark said. "It is good to be a Diplomat. First-rate leaders are well-developed Diplomats *and* well-developed Strategists *and* well-developed Humanitarians."

Lisa nodded her head. "So the idea is not to worry about what your primary category is; the idea is to stay above the line."

"That's exactly right," said John Mark.

"But then," said Lisa, "why label anyone if everyone is a blend of all three categories?"

It was evident to John Mark that Lisa was attempting to justify herself rather than take responsibility for her dark side. But he let her off the hook and answered her without interrogation.

"Let me try to say this more clearly. Although everyone is a mix of all three categories, the model is still helpful because people have inborn tendencies and inclinations," said John Mark. "In my estimation, Lisa, you are more inclined to spend a half hour twisting a conversation than bad-mouthing another person as a Strategist in the basement might do."

She interlocked her fingers and placed her elbows on the arms of the chair. "Okay, I see what you're saying," she said. "But once you fall below the line, how do you get above it once again?"

"That's an excellent question," said John Mark. "One way is by striving to be above the line in the other two categories. You can start to climb out of the Diplomat basement right now—by accepting who you are. Ironically, if you *deny* who you are, you'll fall into the basement automatically."

"It's not so bad to be in the basement if no one knows that you are there," Lisa said, shrugging her shoulders lightly.

John Mark countered, "That's like saying it's not wrong to steal if the person that you're stealing from doesn't know."

"You're stretching the point," said Lisa. "All I'm trying to say is that being in the basement isn't all that big of a deal if you're a benevolent Diplomat who's well-meaning."

"Oh brother," said John Mark.

"You know how much I care about the company," she urged.

"What's your point?" said John Mark.

"I'm raising a practical question. How can anyone compete against all the ruthless people in the business world? You *have* to twist the truth sometimes, John Mark. It's a matter of expediency, a matter of success."

John Mark challenged her with his countenance.

She continued, "Being above the line is a lovely idea, but no one could survive if they seriously tried to do that all the time."

"Lisa, you can't run a gang without having trust as the basis of relationships. Gangbangers may shoot each other, but they don't *always* shoot each other," said John Mark. "Overall, they cooperate with each other and stick together. That's what makes them a gang."

Though Lisa said nothing, John Mark figured she must think he was becoming an idealist.

Ignoring her silence, John Mark continued to argue, "No enterprise is sustainable, even in the short run, if everyone starts falsifying the truth. If you want to win long term, then people absolutely must play as a team. And teamwork is built on trust."

―――――――

Seeing that Lisa wasn't ready to concede his point that the unvarnished truth eventually wins out at the end of the day, John Mark moved on in the conversation. He explained how the three types of people correlate with the three classic types of executive leaders: operational, cultural, and political. Strategists are *operational* leaders, Humanitarians are *cultural* leaders, and Diplomats are *political* leaders.

"Operational leaders," said John Mark, "prioritize solving problems. They can't stand it when the company is disorganized or when people are misaligned, working in jobs that are ill-suited for their skill sets. What they like are strategic plans. Moreover, they're sticklers for meeting deadlines. They want efficiency and effectiveness. Reliable functional systems. Realistic goals. Clarity in the vision. Coherence with the mission. And a sound rationale for all they do.

"Cultural leaders, by contrast, heavily invest in developing the company's ethos. They practically turn the company into a family. They want everyone to feel like they belong. They rehearse the company's history, tell stories, create traditions, and memorialize significant events. Effective cultural leaders can get their people to do almost anything. They motivate people by caring about people. Their way of leading the company is by cultivating a deep sense of ownership and loyalty in every individual who serves as a member of the team.

"In comparison, political leaders lead by collaboration. They unite unlikely forces and pool scarce and limited resources by networking strategically with gatekeepers. They focus more on who than on how. They get things done by mobilizing people to work for a common cause. They elevate people's vision by helping them forget their petty squabbles. Political leaders stir people's imaginations. They offer a sense of hope by painting a beautiful picture of the future."

"That confirms what I said about Max," said Lisa. "As a Humanitarian, he's primarily a cultural leader."

"Yeah, I'd say that's pretty clear," replied John Mark. "Max constantly capitalizes on the company's heritage, and he distributes symbolic tokens at every annual meeting. As a cultural leader, Max puts his focus on people."

"Whereas you're more of an operational leader," said Lisa. "You focus more on truth and the bottom line."

"What would you say about Nathan?" asked John Mark.

"Nathan tends to focus on power," answered Lisa.

"Right," said John Mark. "Political leaders focus on power. And I'll tell you what—the way that power is being distributed in our company right now indicates that Strategists are less valued than Diplomats. Since Strategists tend to ask the tough questions, their voices are sometimes unwelcome."

He looked up at her and remarked, "To say the tough thing is a very tough thing in our company right now because of the political risks."

"You would know," said Lisa.

"And yet," he went on, "what this company might need most is a good Diplomat."

"What's that supposed to mean?" said Lisa.

"Diplomats focus on the timing of things," said John Mark. "Hence, they are invaluable, especially at a time such as this. What may be needed most in our company right now is a well-timed, beautifully articulated, unequivocal message given to Max. Someone has got to clue him in to Nathan's backdoor habit of trying to squeeze himself in by squeezing others out."

"What do you mean by 'backdoor habit'?" Lisa asked.

"I'm saying that Nathan operates by using the back door, not the front door. He negotiates deals on the sly. I don't know exactly what he's up to, but I have a hunch that he's preparing to make a move to squeeze you out."

"Me?" said Lisa. "But how can he? He's not in the inner circle anymore. And why would he? Nathan and I have always been friends. No offense, John Mark, but you're starting to sound a little paranoid."

"I've seen Nathan's patterns," warned John Mark. "It's ridiculous to think he's going to serve behind the scenes quietly and meekly in leadership development. I'd bet my last dollar that Nathan is busy tapping into his network, trying to find a way to maneuver back up the ladder."

"What? You think Max is going to agree to reinstate him?"

"Who said anything about Max reinstating him?" replied John Mark. "You know as well as I do that Nathan has friends on the company's board. Some of them seem to think Nathan hung the moon."

Lisa remarked, "Well then, that probably explains why Max didn't expel Nathan from the company."

"Yes, but it also explains why Nathan didn't quit."

"You think Nathan is sticking around on purpose?"

"I think Nathan has a plan to divide and conquer."

"Whom do you think he's ultimately trying to conquer?"

"The person whose job he wants," replied John Mark.

"You think Nathan wants my job?" asked Lisa.

"I think he wants to be your boss," explained John Mark.

"Then why would he ever want to squeeze me out?"

"Because you're too honest," said John Mark. "Although you're primarily a Diplomat, you're fairly well developed in the Strategist category as well."

"That's crazy," said Lisa.

"It's the Strategist in you that makes you think it's crazy," said John Mark. "Listen to me, Lisa. Starting today, you have access to a new language to describe what's going on. I can say it in one hyphenated word. Ultra-Diplomat. Nathan is an ultra-basement-Diplomat stuck below the line, and his buddies on the board are in the spin club. And good ole Max is sandwiched right between them, scared to death."

John Mark could see that Lisa was concentrating.

"John Mark," she finally said. "On the one hand you make a lot of sense. But at the same time, I can't help but wonder if you might be presuming too much."

He went on, "Lisa, I'm telling you, if you watch, if you wait, and if you use your intuition to sense where various pressures are forcing the power to shift, you'll be able to get a feel for exactly when you need to speak to Max."

"Why lay the burden on me?" said Lisa.

"Because you're primarily a Diplomat," John Mark answered. "You have a good sense of timing, and you're a great networker. You can network your way to the right people in order to obtain the right information so that you can make the right move at the right time. I've watched you, Lisa. You're smooth. Besides, Max likes you."

"Max likes you too," said Lisa.

"Yeah, but a couple of months ago, when he and I were talking, he suggested I try to loosen up a little."

"Loosen up?"

"You know, be more relaxed about things here in the company. Max knows how I jump in with both feet and try to nip problems in the bud. I think he was trying to tell me I can afford to be less urgent."

Lisa responded cordially, "Well, I do think Max likes you quite a lot."

"And I think you're a Diplomat. As I was just saying, you've got what it takes to reach Max."

Upon hearing his affirmation, Lisa voiced a private thought. "Remember the way the e-mail announcement regarding Nathan's reassignment was worded? If the president was in the basement at the time of the announcement, then his message might have been below the line."

"Of course it was," said John Mark. "Instead of strengthening the company culture, the message unsettled the culture. Instead of being crafted with eloquence and finesse, the message was a patchwork of spin."

"Why would Max circumvent the truth?" said Lisa.

"Because that's what people do when they fall below the line," said John Mark. "And Lisa," he added, "Max did more than circumvent the truth. He distorted the truth."

Lisa steered around his criticism and asked, "Do you think Max is more of a Humanitarian-Strategist or a Humanitarian-Diplomat?"

"Hey, I like the idea of doing primary-secondary descriptions," said John Mark. "Well, let's see, I'd say Max is a Humanitarian-Diplomat."

"I agree," said Lisa. "If that's true, then Max simultaneously may have fallen into the basement of the Humanitarians *and* the Diplomats when he sent that message about Nathan 'stepping down.'"

"Speaking of Nathan," said John Mark, "you know what he said to me once? In spite of the fact that he had gone around in public saying that we were 'the premier' company in the industry (even though we weren't), he said to me in private, 'You know, sometime we're going to have to get our act together; I've got a lot of people trusting us these days.'"

Lisa graciously replied, "Well, at least he was aware that a portion of his rhetoric was inflated."

John Mark argued, "Yeah, but he was boasting when he said it."

Lisa responded, "Max says that Nathan is a visionary."

"Do you think that Nathan is a visionary?" said John Mark.

Deflecting the question, Lisa said, "Nathan wasn't the CEO. It wasn't his job to cast a vision for the company."

John Mark tried to persuade her. "What's the difference," he asked, "between a vision and a fantasy? a visionary and a romanticist? a good plan and a grandiose dream?"

"Okay, I get your point."

He went on, "To be a visionary, a leader has to think in terms of the company, the real world, and actual people. Nathan merely thinks in terms of himself."

They sat for a moment in heavy silence. John Mark felt regretful for having slandered Nathan again. But even so, he hoped that Lisa would be persuaded by his perspective.

———

"Hold it," said Lisa, easing the tension. "Isn't there an overlap in the Humanitarians' basement and the Diplomats' basement? I don't see the difference between people pleasing and image management."

John Mark nodded his head. "Let me back up for a second. I should have told you before that it's helpful to think of the model in terms of grammar: first person, second person, and third person. The Strategists are oriented toward second-person thinking. Since they tend to be corrective, they think in terms of *you*: what *you* need to know, what *you* need to do, what *you* need to correct, what *you* need to agree with, etc.

"The Humanitarians are oriented toward third-person thinking. Since they tend to be people developers, they think in terms

VIEWPOINT:	2nd Person (You) —Operational	3rd Person (He, She, They) —Cultural	1st Person (I, We) —Political
	STRATEGISTS (Light)	HUMANITARIANS (Temp)	DIPLOMATS (Color)
	Freedom	Compassion	Peace
	Authentic Community	Comfortable Community	Impressive Community
	Be Good	Feel Good	Look Good
	Clarity, Accountability	Develop, Support People	Sense of Harmony and Order
	Integrity	Togetherness	Unity
	Straightforward Message	Wise Approach	Wise Timing
	Confrontational	Forbearing	Nonconfrontational
	Discerning, Analytical	Patient, Kind	Finesse, Artful Demeanor
	Corrective	Loyal	Polished, Refined
	Self-Righteous	Self-Serving	Self-Absorbed
	Criticism, Harshness	People Pleasing	Image Management
BEHAVIOR:	Self-Righteous Judgment —Slander —Presumption —Impatience	Enablement —Gossip —Guilt Trips —Martyr Complex	Spin (Spin Club) —Distorts, Redefines Truth —Political Intimidation —Victim of Circumstances

of *he, she,* and *they*: how *he* is feeling, what *she* needs in order to grow, what *they* need to have done for them, etc.

"The Diplomats are oriented toward first-person thinking. Since they tend to be concerned about public relations, they think in terms of *I* and *we*: what *I* should do to position myself; what *we*, as a company, should tell the public about ourselves, etc.

"Do you see where I'm headed?" he said. "The Humanitarians try to please people because they want people (he, she, they) to like them. Essentially they're self-serving when in the basement. But when leading above the line, a Humanitarian wants them—the people being led—to prosper and thrive."

He added, "Diplomats try to please people too, but they do so from a different motivation. They want to build good will because they know how advantageous it is to have a good reputation. Below-the-line Diplomats don't care about making other people happy per se. Below-the-line Diplomats are more interested in promoting themselves. They want the company to succeed (that's the *we*) because in their minds, corporate success ultimately accrues to themselves (that's the *I*)."

"I'm glad I asked," said Lisa. "That clarifies a lot for me. But I've got to tell you, John Mark, I'm not sure I see this situation with Nathan as being as black-and-white as you do. And I still don't really see why Nathan is my problem. Furthermore, I suspect that if I bring it up with Max, I'll be misunderstood and come across as a meddler."

As she looked again at the chart, John Mark conceded that Lisa wasn't ready to talk openly with Max, much less reveal the truth about Nathan.

CHAPTER 7

THREE ASPECTS
OF A COMPANY

Over two hours had elapsed since John Mark and Lisa had begun their meeting. Yet the afternoon still felt young because both of them were enthralled by the People Model. They ordered two bottles of Perrier and resumed the conversation.

Lisa said, "Since everyone is a mix of all three categories, then it must be the case that everyone falls into all three basements sometimes."

"It happens," said John Mark. "Believe me, I've been in all three basements simultaneously before."

"What did that look like?" said Lisa.

"Back when I first started in the workplace," said John Mark, "I was scared to displease my boss because I was terribly concerned to prove myself. I worked furiously to win her approval, and I tried even harder to come across as though I wasn't afraid."

"That covers the lower story of the Humanitarian and Diplomat columns," said Lisa. "How did you fall below the line in the Strategist column?"

"I started feeling angry at the boss."

"Why?" said Lisa.

"Because her standards seemed arbitrary. She was fickle. One day she wanted one thing, and another day she wanted something else. I got really mad at her because she was making it so difficult for me to prove that I could please her. I griped behind her back all the time."

Lisa smiled at him warmly. "Then what?"

"I suffered," said John Mark. "Believe me, those were hard years. I put myself through so much unnecessary turmoil. Nevertheless, I kept telling myself that I could take it, that I could triumph no matter what."

"How long did that season last?"

"Five long years," said John Mark. "Almost six years, in fact."

"So how did you break the cycle?" asked Lisa.

"I confronted my boss."

"What did you say to her?" Lisa inquired.

"I told her that I was afraid."

"How did you get the courage to do that?"

"I don't know," said John Mark. "I think I finally got tired of wasting my energy worrying about my image. It seemed so unstrategic to me."

"How did your boss respond?" said Lisa.

"At first, she didn't really understand," said John Mark. "She thought I was scared of being fired. But the fear of losing my job was not my fear. My fear was that I wouldn't appear successful."

Lisa laughed and said, "I can understand that."

John Mark continued, "Then I told her something else."

"Yeah?" said Lisa. "What was that?"

"I told her that I didn't respect her."

"You *said* that to her?" said Lisa.

"Yes, I told her that instead of respecting her, I had fallen into a trap of trying to meet her every expectation."

"How does that relate to disrespecting her?" asked Lisa.

"Had I respected her," said John Mark, "I would've been able to accept her expressions of displeasure as indications of her problems, not mine. I would have respected her for having her own frustrations. Instead, I personalized her frustrations. Whenever I sensed that she was frustrated, I assumed she was frustrated with me."

"That's deep," said Lisa.

"Yes, but it was healing for me once I figured it out," said John Mark.

"So then what did you do?"

"I apologized for disrespecting her."

"You apologized?" asked Lisa.

"Yes, I told her I was sorry for investing too much energy in trying to please her. Then I confessed to myself that I had been more interested in winning her approval than in using my best judgment in decision making."

"And that cured your anger?" Lisa asked.

"It did," said John Mark. "Once I decided to relax and be myself, I didn't feel angry anymore. In other words, when I took ownership of *my* problem, I was able to dismiss *her* problem."

"That's great," said Lisa.

"Yeah, and after that, I became more effective," said John Mark. "A month or two later, my boss promoted me to be director of operations. It was a small company, but I got great experience. A few years later, I came here."

"Wow," Lisa responded. "You learned a lot at a young age."

"I'm still learning a lot now," said John Mark. "For one thing, I'm learning about the People Model. Can I show you something?"

John Mark slid a pencil behind his ear and then explained, "Look at this. There's an inherent logic to the model. Let me try to illustrate what I mean. The People Model implies that the Strategists are spirited, the Humanitarians are gentle, and the Diplomats are calm."

He tilted the chart toward Lisa, covering all but the upstairs of the Strategist category.

"Okay, let's look at this. Truth is represented by light. Once you understand that light exposes, it becomes self-evident that light brings clarity to a given situation. Clarity paves the way for holding people accountable, and accountability creates the need for correction. Correction, in turn, gives way to confrontation. It's really no surprise, then, that Strategists tend to be spirited. They're spirited because they're confrontational."

He pulled the pencil out from behind his ear and said, "Notice where I'm writing on the chart. I'm putting the word *spirited* in the far left column beside the word *confrontational* and just above the word set *discerning* and *analytical*. See what else the People Model implies? It shows that Strategists are spirited because they're discerning and analytical. It's only natural for them to get riled up. Strategists are spirited because they're able to identify real problems and solutions."

Lisa inadvertently laughed. She had certainly seen the spirited side of John Mark. One time he got so fired up after identifying a problem that he took thirty people, including a dozen secretaries, out to celebrate over lunch. At the restaurant, one of the salespeople at John Mark's table stood up and asked, "Hey, Boss, why are we celebrating? We didn't even solve the problem yet!"

VIEWPOINT:	2nd Person (You) —Operational	3rd Person (He, She, They) —Cultural	1st Person (I, We) —Political
	STRATEGISTS (Light)	**HUMANITARIANS** (Temp)	**DIPLOMATS** (Color)
	Freedom	Compassion	Peace
	Authentic Community	Comfortable Community	Impressive Community
	Be Good	Feel Good	Look Good
	Clarity, Accountability	Develop, Support People	Sense of Harmony and Order
	Integrity	Togetherness	Unity
	Straightforward Message	Wise Approach	Wise Timing
	Confrontational, *Spirited*	Forbearing	Nonconfrontational
	Discerning, Analytical	Patient, Kind	Finesse, Artful Demeanor
	Corrective	Loyal	Polished, Refined

John Mark raised his glass and answered with a toast. "To *identifying* the problem," he said. "Now that we've found the problem, we can get it solved." Everyone tipped their glasses and cheered. That was the John Mark whom everybody loved. That was John Mark at his best.

She listened as he continued. "Now consider the Humanitarians' column. Goodness is represented by a comfortable temperature, and a comfortable temperature feels nice. It feels nice to be supported. Nice to have a sense of belonging. It feels pleasant to be showered with compassion. Do you see the inner logic? The Humanitarians are gentle precisely because they're patient and kind and forbearing."

He wrote the word *gentle* in the middle column beside the word *forbearing*.

Then he explained the inner logic in the Diplomats' column.

"Diplomacy, as we know, is represented by color—that is, by

VIEWPOINT:	2nd Person (You) —Operational	3rd Person (He, She, They) —Cultural	1st Person (I, We) —Political
	STRATEGISTS (Light)	**HUMANITARIANS** (Temp)	**DIPLOMATS** (Color)
	Freedom	Compassion	Peace
	Authentic Community	Comfortable Community	Impressive Community
	Be Good	Feel Good	Look Good
	Clarity, Accountability	Develop, Support People	Sense of Harmony and Order
	Integrity	Togetherness	Unity
	Straightforward Message	Wise Approach	Wise Timing
	Confrontational, Spirited	Forbearing, *Gentle*	Nonconfrontational
	Discerning, Analytical	Patient, Kind	Finesse, Artful Demeanor
	Corrective	Loyal	Polished, Refined

the concept of beauty. It is hardly a beautiful thing to be confrontational. One has to be calm if one is to comport oneself with poise and refinement. It's virtually self-evident on the basis of logic that Diplomats are intentionally nonconfrontational. The word *calm*, therefore, belongs beside the word *nonconfrontational* and above the words *finesse* and *artful demeanor.*

"Does that make sense?" asked John Mark.

"Yes, very much so," said Lisa.

"Great, then I'll keep going," said John Mark. "The model's internal logic says that the Strategists care about building the company *infrastructure*; the Humanitarians major in *service*; and the Diplomats put their focus on *public relations.*"

He went on, "See how the model interconnects? Strategists build the infrastructure for the sake of integrity; Humanitarians lend their services for the sake of togetherness; and Diplomats attend to public relations for the sake of overall unity. If you really want to think big picture, you can see this concept embedded in the structure of the three branches of the United States government. The Diplomats are the executive branch—unifying the people and doing public relations abroad. The Humanitarians are the legislative branch—making laws for the people and serving them by voicing their concerns. The Strategists are the judicial branch, holding everyone accountable and ensuring that our infrastructure accords with the American Constitution. The Founding Fathers designed the three powers to regulate and balance one another.

"Okay now, did you catch it?" he asked. "There's a parallel here to the business community."

Lisa waited for him to explain.

VIEWPOINT:	2nd Person (You) —Operational	3rd Person (He, She, They) —Cultural	1st Person (I, We) —Political
	STRATEGISTS (Light)	**HUMANITARIANS** (Temp)	**DIPLOMATS** (Color)
	Freedom	Compassion	Peace
	Authentic Community	Comfortable Community	Impressive Community
	Be Good	Feel Good	Look Good
	Clarity, Accountability	Develop, Support People	Sense of Harmony and Order
	Integrity	Togetherness	Unity
	Straightforward Message	Wise Approach	Wise Timing
	Confrontational, Spirited	Forbearing, Gentle	Nonconfrontational, **Calm**
	Discerning, Analytical	Patient, Kind	Finesse, Artful Demeanor
	Corrective	Loyal	Polished, Refined
PRIORITY:	**INFRASTRUCTURE**	**SERVICE**	**PUBLIC RELATIONS**

"Every business is more likely to succeed if proper emphasis is placed on infrastructure, service, and PR. When that emphasis *doesn't* happen in each of these three areas, the company runs into problems because the company becomes imbalanced.

"For instance, if you're all about infrastructure, and you overemphasize protocol, process, and quality, then you end up losing sales. It's ridiculous to perfect a system of production if in doing so, you practically tell the customer to go away. Customers want to feel valued. Likewise, if you become too internally focused and so nitpicky that you obsess about the quality, the public will forget *you* because you will have already forgotten them.

"But if you're all about public relations and all you ever do is spend money on making friends and creating the perception that you're better than you are, you end up going broke. Either you get the customers (by glitter and persuasion) and then fall into the first scenario where there's no supporting infrastructure, or you never get the customers at all because they find out from the get-go that you have a lousy service or shoddy product.

"On the other hand, if service is overprioritized, then you end up with more customers than the infrastructure is able to sustain. It doesn't take long before you've enraged a mass of people and wrecked your reputation for good service."

Lisa responded, "You're saying that it's best to build a well-balanced company of Strategists, Humanitarians, and Diplomats."

John Mark clarified, "Yes, and here's how you do that. You deliberately create Strategist job descriptions and Humanitarian job descriptions and Diplomat job descriptions.

"In other words," he said, "you pay people to value one thing over another. You pay the service people to prioritize service. You pay the quality people to prioritize quality. And you pay the

PR workers to prioritize the task of managing the company's reputation."

"But that will lead to conflict," Lisa stated.

"Yes," said John Mark. "Conflict is the force that balances the powers within the company. Without conflict, one side will dominate the other two."

"You think conflict is fundamental to success?" asked Lisa.

"Yes, I do," said John Mark. "But you have to have the *right kind* of conflict. You don't let people argue about whether to honor the truth or whether to steward your reputation or whether to value people in the company. What you do is pay people to *prioritize* one of these core values while understanding all three are important. I mean, it'd be great if everyone could value all three aspects of the company with equal zeal, but I don't think that's very realistic. I think it's more advisable to hire a CEO who can bring together a team of capable vice presidents who champion the three aspects of a company.

"Let me cite a few examples," he continued. "If anyone at the top devalues truth, then the company's quality will slip. Similarly, if compassion is devalued, then the company's service will be worse. And if those at the top underestimate the importance of people's perceptions, there will be a problem with public relations. So the moral of the story is for people at the top to value all three types. The last thing you want is to stack the executive team with one category."

Lisa asked, "What do you think would happen if an executive team *was* stacked with people who were primarily of the same category?"

John Mark couldn't wait to answer the question.

"I've thought about that," he said.

He scooted back his chair to give himself more space.

"I believe it's risky to lead with an imbalanced team. A team comprised exclusively of Strategists, for instance, might potentially produce the greatest results. But if they fall below the line, collectively they might share the same presumptions, and presumptions quickly harden into prejudice.

"Let me put it this way. When a group of basement Strategists lead on the basis of their prejudice, they will tend to scapegoat everyone who disagrees with them. Indeed, groups of basement Strategists can be lethal—even when their presumptions are dissimilar—because in that case, they start fighting each other. Below-the-line Strategists are famous for dividing into hair-splitting factions. Of course, this problem comes about because Strategists in the basement tend to bluster rather than listen or discuss.

"Something similar can be said about the Humanitarians. A team composed exclusively of Humanitarians will probably build the strongest community. But if they fall below the line, they might try too hard to please too many people. As a result, they will tend to work too much. And I said before, when a group of Humanitarians start leading from the basement, the next thing you know they start to label as 'disloyal' those workers who refuse to overwork.

"To their credit, Humanitarians are service oriented, yet to their detriment, they're quite vulnerable to forgetting the company's mission. Because of their proclivity to want to service everyone, they also end up stalling at the decision-making table—which causes further problems and complications."

Switching categories, he said, "If you stack a team exclusively with Diplomats, you'll probably have the most impressive company. But if they fall below the line, you'll also have a group of warring egos. Egos, by nature, tend to clash with one another irrespectively. No doubt, on the surface these Diplomats will be smiling. Secretly, however, they'll be stabbing each other's backs behind the scenes. Everyone on the team will tend to shirk responsibility for problems that might cause embarrassment. Instead of solving problems, they will probably bury them and just hope they'll go away over time.

"So there you have it," said John Mark. "When clusters of people from the same category fall down into the basement, their ability to lead well is impoverished. That's why my theory is this—that a first-rate leader and a first-rate team will always be a mix of all three."

As the conversation drew to a close, Lisa asked John Mark if she could keep his copy of the chart. After he handed it to her, both of them walked back to their cars. As John Mark returned to his office, all he could think about was rising above the line in all three categories.

CHAPTER 8

TAKING
INVENTORY

It was Friday evening. Cynthia was at the hospital working the evening shift, so John Mark was alone. Though usually he would have chosen to relax, his meeting with Lisa had stimulated his thinking, particularly with regard to the elements that lie below the line. It had bugged him for months that he hadn't found a way to live above the line consistently.

By way of review, he acknowledged to himself once again that the contents in the basement are interconnected. That is, the elements in each category are conceptually related to one another. For instance, in the Strategist category, criticism and slander are linked. He also remembered the link between presumption and impatience.

John Mark sat thinking to himself. *To presume is to tell*

	STRATEGISTS (Light)	HUMANITARIANS (Temp)	DIPLOMATS (Color)
	Self-Righteous	Self-Serving	Self-Absorbed
	Criticism, Harshness	People Pleasing	Image Management
BEHAVIOR:	Self-Righteous Judgment	Enablement	Spin (Spin Club)
	—Slander	—Gossip	—Distorts, Redefines Truth
	—Presumption	—Guilt Trips	—Political Intimidation
	—Impatience	—Martyr Complex	—Victim of Circumstances

myself, "I know this already." To presume is to decide that listening isn't important or strategic. To presume is to be impatient. Presumption is the enemy of listening, and impatience is presumption's twin sister.

He remembered how impatience had derailed him temporarily about six years earlier. It had caused him to blow up at the team of salespeople he was managing. They had fallen behind on quotas and then presented him with a litany of excuses. He had been angry because he knew what the team needed to do. After all, he had fulfilled his portion of the quotas. By John Mark's calculations, the failure of the team had cost the company millions.

A recent article came to mind. The chief executive officers from the top companies in the world had been interviewed. When questioned, every CEO who was interviewed said that listening was by far the greatest component of the job. Independent of each other, each leader estimated that the vast majority of his time was specifically devoted to listening. The article hit him hard. He had been trained to speak—and he could do that well. But he had not been formally trained to be a listener.

Somewhere along the line John Mark had been taught that listening requires empathy. But John Mark was better at thinking than feeling. He typically preferred for people to just get to the point.

John Mark reflected further. *How many times have I failed to double-check that communication lines are clear? How many times have I acted too quickly without getting enough input from my team? How many times have I pretended to be listening when I wasn't? How many times have I frustrated other people by listening to—but not hearing—what they said? That's the very problem with presumption. When you do it, you don't know it.*

John Mark didn't want to be presumptuous. He didn't want to be a bad listener. He didn't want to jump to conclusions prematurely.

A myriad of details clamored in his mind. Among the most indicting was the vague recollection that he had failed to exercise enough managerial patience to coach the sales team, to walk *with* them, and to help them work smarter. He wondered, *Did I really do my part as the leader? Or did I presume that the members of the team should have known how to succeed without my help?*

It agitated him to think of this. He cleared his throat and released the pent-up air that pressurized his lungs. Then he directed his attention to the next category.

Looking at the elements in the basement of the Humanitarians, he said to himself out loud, "People pleasing. Who doesn't want to please people? You'd have to be a sociopath to be free from falling prey to this temptation."

Whipping out a piece of scratch paper, he brainstormed several ways that people pleasing typically plays out.

- *Saying what you think other people want to hear*
- *Feeling guilty for disagreeing with a superior*

- *Being guided more by people than sound principles of right and wrong*
- *Telling white lies for the sake of "not hurting someone's feelings"*
- *Taking things too personally*

The People Model nailed him once again. Just the day before he had taken to heart—taken too personally—something his wife Cynthia had carelessly said in passing. Cognitively he realized that her words were reflective mostly of her work frustrations, yet he had let her comments get under his skin, and they had had a tiff as a result.

Next, he contemplated the elements below the line in the Diplomat category. *Self-absorption.* He paused to ruminate. *Somehow self-absorption leads to deceitfulness and lies.*

John Mark was stumped. Intuitively he knew that focusing on the self blinds a human being to the self. But John Mark couldn't see exactly why.

"Hmmm," he pondered. Then the answer came to him.

"Self-absorption is itself a form of delusion," he announced, "because it overlooks the fact that other people matter as much as I do. Self-absorption is a form of conceit."

He decided to make a list of the kinds of public images he had projected in the past.

- *That I am a winner*
- *That I am not afraid*
- *That I can always be trusted to tell the truth*

Scanning through the bullet points, he scrutinized each one. He started with the first: *That I am a winner.*

Yes, he had won competitions before—he was high school salutatorian; he graduated cum laude from Harvard; he had trophies for tennis and soccer; and he had been top salesperson of the year. But he had lost more competitions than he had won. He didn't win valedictorian; he didn't graduate summa cum laude; he had lost the majority of all the tennis and soccer tournaments he had entered; and he was only the top salesperson for three of seven years on the job.

He went on to the second: *That I am not afraid.*

I'm not afraid of my job, he acknowledged to himself, *but I'm definitely afraid of some other things.*

He noted, partly in amusement, partly in serious reflection— *I'm scared of terrorists, the IRS, my mother-in-law, and the thought of personal failure. I also feel afraid whenever I imagine what might happen to me and my family when I die.*

Then to the third: *That I can always be trusted to tell the truth.*

"That one is the most insidious," he mused aloud, "since it's the biggest facade I try to project."

Though in his heart John Mark knew he was mostly faithful to his wife, mostly honest in his taxes, and mostly ethical in his work, he also understood that he wasn't completely faithful or honest. He could be a chameleon and politick his way around the office ("Great idea," he had said about ideas that were plainly mediocre); he could fudge in a business meeting now and then ("Sorry I have to leave early," he had said before leaving to play golf); and he could easily exaggerate when telling complimentary stories about himself ("I kid you not—this guy was *not* going to buy from anyone! So when I landed the sale . . .").

Needless to say, he was very familiar with the Diplomats' downstairs. John Mark definitely had it in him to cast the limelight on himself, artfully display his clever wit, slip in boastful statements, sprinkle in self-deprecating jokes, and revise whatever story he was telling by adding just enough of a twist to make the story sound truer than it was.

At this point, John Mark's musings screeched to a halt. Overwhelmed by the endless task of soul-searching, he bellowed out the sixty-four-thousand-dollar question, "So what?! So what about the basement! Everybody's in the basement sometimes. What's the point in wasting time delineating the obvious—I'm not perfect, and no one else is perfect!"

It wasn't John Mark's nature to despair. But his stubborn sense of realism made it hard for him to minimize the actual consequences—the steep cost of being a leader below the line. *How much had it cost the company to put up with Nathan, for instance?*

More broadly, he wondered, *How staggering is the cost of the company's basement choices all combined?*

He thought about the cost of his own presumption. He recalled in detail a particular miscommunication that had occurred between himself and a major customer. At the time, he was convinced that the customer had lied. As it turned out, the customer had simply been unclear. John Mark, however, had interpreted the customer's statements strictly in accordance with his own personal understanding of the deal. To make a long story short, the cost of the miscommunication translated into three weeks of extra work, a strained relationship with the customer for a month, and a temporary loss of John Mark's personal sense of well-being . . . not to mention the added tension that leaked into his family life and marriage.

That was it. He was going to war against the basement. Stirred by renewed motivation, he abandoned his comfortable chair, physically dropped to the floor, and pumped out fifty push-ups. Then he sprang up from the carpet, dashed to the kitchen, swung open the refrigerator door, grabbed a bottle of water, and chugged it down.

"Okay, I got this baby figured out."

Once again, he placed the full chart in front of him and inserted three new words into the model: *pride, fear,* and *deceitfulness.*

With a single clap, he said, "Here's the deal. The People Model is a tool for increasing self-awareness.

VIEWPOINT:	2nd Person (You) —Operational	3rd Person (He, She, They) —Cultural	1st Person (I, We) —Political
	STRATEGISTS (Light)	**HUMANITARIANS** (Temp)	**DIPLOMATS** (Color)
	Freedom	Compassion	Peace
	Authentic Community	Comfortable Community	Impressive Community
	Be Good	Feel Good	Look Good
	Clarity, Accountability	Develop, Support People	Sense of Harmony and Order
	Integrity	Togetherness	Unity
	Straightforward Message	Wise Approach	Wise Timing
	Confrontational, Spirited	Forbearing, Gentle	Nonconfrontational, Calm
	Discerning, Analytical	Patient, Kind	Finesse, Artful Demeanor
	Corrective	Loyal	Polished, Refined
PRIORITY:	INFRASTRUCTURE	SERVICE	PUBLIC RELATIONS
	Self-Righteous	Self-Serving	Self-Absorbed
	Criticism, Harshness	People Pleasing	Image Management
BEHAVIOR:	Self-Righteous Judgment —Slander —Presumption —Impatience	Enablement —Gossip —Guilt Trips —Martyr Complex	Spin (Spin Club) —Distorts, Redefines Truth —Political Intimidation —Victim of Circumstances
THE PROBLEM:	**PRIDE**	**FEAR**	**DECEITFULNESS**

"The Strategists—the clarity crowd, the accountability crew, the sticklers for integrity—they're like me. They're analytical, which is good, and critical, which is bad. They're discerning, which is helpful, and self-righteously judgmental, which is destructive. They're confrontal, which is good, yet impatient, which is bad; they might do well to pause before advancing a confrontation. They're authentic, which is good, but they slander, which is bad. In a word, their problem boils down to *pride*.

"As for the Humanitarians, they're more like Max and Cynthia. They're compassionate and kind, but they put up with too much garbage. They're forbearing, which is good, but they're enabling, which is bad. They're patient, which is good, but too tolerant, which is bad. They're gentle and considerate, but too timid when it comes to handling conflict. They're loyal and servant oriented, but they're willing to be martyrs when they should draw a boundary instead. They're people developers, but sometimes they gossip, even about the folks they're trying to help. They want everyone to feel comfortable, yet they're prone to feeling guilty because they're too concerned with pleasing people. In a word, the Humanitarians' problem distills into the problem of *fear.*

"As for the Diplomats, they're like Lisa and Nathan: peacemakers, unity-builders, and creators of harmony, and yet they compromise excessively when in the basement. They're willing to give up too much for the sake of a mere perception of harmonious order. They're winsome, which is good, but they're vain, which is bad. They're calm, which is good, but they're aloof, which is bad—because they tend to be absorbed with themselves. They're skillful with finesse, but they can use their finesse to artfully spin a story that isn't true. They sound credible and attractive—whether through humor or intelligence or charisma—but they're prone to solicit pity rather than owning up to their own junk. At their best, they're politically astute, but at their worst, they're politically corrupt. In a word, the core problem with the Diplomats is *deceitfulness.*"

The power of the People Model was settling upon him. It stretched him far beyond his normal analytical way of thinking. It stirred in him a desire to be bold and authentic like a Strategist, kind and empathetic like a Humanitarian, winsome and peacemaking like a Diplomat. Instead of causing him to be guarded and defensive, the People Model made him want to change. It motivated him in a special kind of way because it offered him a glimpse of his potential.

He fell asleep on the couch with the People Model chart crumpled under his arm, but his thoughts remained in motion nonetheless. In the middle of the night, he had a dream about his college days at Harvard. He could vaguely feel himself reaching for some thoughts that were buried in the back of his mind. He got up and went to the bathroom, then jotted down on his chart some preliminary thoughts about the practical solutions the People Model inherently suggests.

Forty minutes later, he faded back into his slumber.

CHAPTER 9

HIDING YOUR TRASH OR NOT

The next morning, Cynthia found her husband lying next to her in bed. He had groggily trudged upstairs after waking up on the couch a second time.

Though it was only seven o'clock, Cynthia had been thinking for two hours. As soon as John Mark awakened, she gazed at him and said something that she normally wouldn't say.

"I want to be a better person," she remarked.

"What makes you say that?" asked John Mark.

"That People Model of yours is getting to me."

"Tell me about it," he said, smirking. "It kept me up past midnight, then woke me up two more times."

Cynthia chuckled. "You were snoring on the couch when I came home."

"I must have had a dream or something because I was thinking about Harvard for some reason."

He turned toward his wife.

"Tell me a little more. You want to be a better person in what way?"

"I don't like the thought of being in the basement," she replied. "Life is too short to spend time worrying as much as I do. For years I've concerned myself with far too many things."

John Mark responded by bringing her up to speed on the progress he had made the night before. Then he told her that the root problem in the downstairs of the Humanitarians is fear.

"So the antidote for you, my love, is courage," he concluded.

"But how can I gain courage?" Cynthia asked.

"You imitate the lion in *The Wizard of Oz*."

"I forget what he did," she replied.

"He gained courage by traveling to Oz. He got it by going forward on a journey. It was the *going* that gave him courage. The wizard didn't give the lion anything, except that realization."

"Oh yeah," said Cynthia. "So how do I get going? What does that mean practically in my life?"

"To begin with," said John Mark, "you take inventory. You sit down and get real honest about your strengths and weaknesses. Then you figure out what changes you'd like to make."

"Have you done that yourself?" Cynthia asked.

"I've invested hours."

"You've cataloged your weaknesses?"

"Yep," said John Mark, "that's what I was doing last night—taking inventory of my trash, that is, my flaws."

"What about your strengths? Have you taken time to enumerate them too?" said Cynthia.

"Not really, but I know them," he answered.

"What are they?" She propped herself up against the pillows.

"You want me to say them right now?"

"Yes, you go first, and then I'll go after you," she suggested.

John Mark rattled off his answer: "Let's see, my strengths lie in analytical skills, communication skills, persuasion, and making people feel excited and inspired. I tend to be pretty good at getting people to deal with problems. And I'm a workhorse; I never ask my people to work any harder than I do. That's a decent summary of my strengths."

"And what about your weaknesses?" she asked.

"I'm presumptuous, impatient, and slow to empathize," said John Mark. "I have a hard time being calm, unless there's a crisis and I'm the one in charge."

He paused, then added, "And I'm just not smooth when I'm angry. You should hear what I said to Lisa about Nathan. Talk about being in the basement. I can crank out the slander, no problem."

"Well, then, what are the main changes that you would like to make in yourself?" asked Cynthia.

"I want to learn to pause before speaking my mind. I also want to pause before cementing my opinions. If I can do those two things, I believe I'll be more calm and diplomatic."

Cynthia tilted her head and offered a comforting smile. A few seconds later, she said, "Okay, here's what I really want to know. How are you going to change? What's the actual process of rising above the line?"

"I'll tell what the answer is not," said John Mark. "The answer is *not* that I will simply try harder.

"I won't be any calmer," he went on to explain, "if I merely put forth the effort to be calm. What will help me succeed is to focus instead on implementing the Diplomats' solution."

"What's the Diplomats' solution?" asked Cynthia.

John Mark answered, "The Diplomats' solution is to submit to the canons of good timing and operate more indirectly. Oftentimes a bank shot, so to speak, is more effective than a straight shot aimed directly at the hoop. Sometimes it's better to finesse things than to fix them right away."

"Now you're talking specifics," Cynthia stated. "This is good."

"But it's hard for me to lean into the Diplomats' solution. I'm more naturally attracted toward the Strategists' solution."

"What's the Strategists' solution?" she asked.

"To fix it! To just get in there and fix it by the power of the will—and the blood, sweat, and tears of hard work. You know me, Cynthia, I'm a doer. I'll read the books, lift the weights, jog the miles, take the classes, attend the conferences, work the hours, learn the new technology, and so forth."

"You do like to have things fixed," she agreed. "I think that's why I'm afraid sometimes to tell you about my trash. I'm worried you'll just try to clear it out."

John Mark responded sincerely, "I don't want to be too demanding."

Cynthia looked down.

"Honestly, I want to be more supportive," he said.

"You're supportive in your own way," she affirmed.

"But I want to be *more* supportive from now on."

John Mark could see the ambivalence in her face. Did she not believe him? Or was it dawning on her that if he was more supportive, she could no longer blame him for her shortcomings?

"It's basically pretty easy to support you," he assured her, "because you're honest enough to identify your trash. What drives me nuts is when people want to be accepted exactly as they are without admitting or trying to change their character flaws."

"But don't you think most people already have an idea of where they might be missing the mark?"

"Overall, I do not," he answered flatly.

"Then why do you think people routinely feel guilty and anxious?" Cynthia argued.

"You're projecting," said John Mark. "You're the one who feels unsettled by your choices. I can guarantee you that many, many people feel *entitled* to their choices. They think they have the *right* to do whatever they please whenever they want."

"You're wrong," Cynthia countered. "People *do* have a sense of where they're missing the mark. The problem is they don't know how to change. They're defensive and unyielding because inside they feel defeated."

"Cynthia, that's illogical. Of course, you'll feel defeated if you refuse to take steps forward. That's tantamount to saying that people feel defeated whenever they decide to defeat themselves."

"It's a matter of emotions, not cognition," she said. "I hate to say it, John Mark, but sometimes you act as though everything in life is bound to the principles of logic. I wish you could see that people give up on meeting high standards whenever they feel defeated from the get-go."

Part of John Mark wanted to set his wife straight. (He really did have a logical point—just because you *feel* defeated doesn't mean that you *are* defeated.) But he posed a personal question instead.

"Do you feel defeated?" he asked.

"I don't know," she answered. "I guess I feel like hiding my negative feelings."

"Why hide them?" he asked, trying to fix his wife. "Hiding won't make your feelings go away."

"Then what's the solution?"

"The Strategists' solution!" said John Mark. He grabbed a piece of paper and started writing.

"Wait," said Cynthia. "I thought you said the Strategists' solution is to fix things. How does that apply here?"

"The Strategists' solution is more involved than that," he explained. "First, you have to value truth enough to admit your actual guilt and take responsibility for your trash. It's okay to feel guilty if you really are guilty. But guilt becomes destructive when you continue to hang on to it or assume it when it belongs to someone else.

"Second," he said, "you have to value your own integrity over and above pleasing people."

"I value people more than anything," Cynthia claimed.

"If you really value people, then you will honor their dignity," said John Mark.

He went on, "When you fall into the basement, what you value, Cynthia, is *pleasing* people. That is quite different from valuing individuals and calling out the best they can be."

"I don't like the idea of putting pressure on people," Cynthia argued.

"Pressure can be a good thing," John Mark stated, "if it's noble, positive pressure. Look at the business world. Every CEO will perform a little better if the board puts positive pressure on him or her. It's impossible to be a first-rate leader if all you want to do is relax. Exertion itself requires pressure—pressure from within and pressure from without. It takes pressure to produce positive changes."

"But pressure can feel like punishment," Cynthia countered.

"And in that case, it's not good," agreed John Mark. "Punishment pushes people further below the line. People need discipline, not punishment. Consequences, not punishment. Positive pressure, not punishment.

"It's similar to raising kids," he continued. "You give the kid a choice. For example, you say, 'Okay, if you clean up your room, then you can play on the computer for a while. But if you *don't* clean up your room, then you'll have to face the consequences. And the consequence for having a messy room means that you don't get to play. So make your choice, and then you can evaluate whether or not you like how your choice turns out.'

"The very same principle applies to adults in the business world. You give your workers choices, and you set up proper rewards and consequences. Then you constantly make sure that everyone understands exactly what they're being asked to do."

"Okay, let me make sure I've got this," said Cynthia. "There's a difference between pleasing people and helping people. If you try to please people by compromising the truth or forfeiting your integrity, then you're really not helping people at all."

"That's right," said John Mark.

"You know what?" said Cynthia in a vulnerable tone of voice. "Part of my trash is that I don't like to have positive pressure placed on me."

"That's why you're afraid to put it on others," said John Mark.

Cynthia slid her fingers along her jaw. It was hard for her to hear her husband say this. But John Mark didn't let up.

"You could help people more if you wouldn't always coddle them. You could help them more by challenging them to exercise their dignity."

Then he added, "But you have to be convinced of this. Otherwise, you won't exercise the courage that you need."

Cynthia had a sudden breakthrough.

"Oh my goodness!" she exclaimed. "If I honestly believe in the dignity of people, I'll be able to call them to higher standards. I always feel so bad for other people. And I usually feel afraid that people won't believe that I truly care about them if I counter them or challenge their decisions."

"See?" said John Mark. "You're worried about yourself. You care more about yourself than other people."

Cynthia groaned, "Ahhgh! I hate it when you pound on me right when I'm confessing my struggles!"

John Mark reacted by springing from the bed and pacing around the room.

"I wasn't pounding you," he said, trying to persuade Cynthia that he was right. "I'm trying to help you see what's going on."

"I know, but you make it so painful for me to cooperate," she said. "I would do better if you would be more sensitive to my feelings." She wanted more than anything for her husband to enable her behavior.

John Mark exhaled.

"Well, if it's any consolation," he said, rising above the line, "I do want to be more empathetic."

Cynthia's heart was softened.

"Help me," he said. "How can I be more empathetic?"

"When you empathize," said Cynthia, "you listen to the feelings that the other person feels. You listen to their emotions, not their thoughts."

"Like how?" said John Mark.

"Like when Nathan used to tell you about his grandiose plans," she answered. "You could've empathized with him. You could have said, 'Nathan, you sound really excited about what we could accomplish.'"

"And egg him on?!" said John Mark in a flabbergasted tone.

"See? Right there!" said Cynthia. "Right there your inclination was to assume the worst and try to fix him."

"For his own benefit!" exclaimed John Mark.

"But you didn't try to validate his emotions," she explained.

"Why should I? He's deluded!" said John Mark.

"If you empathize with people, you can tap into their wavelength," she said.

John Mark was arrested by her word choice. For months he had attempted to make a concerted effort to do just that—tap into Nathan's wavelength. But he still couldn't lower his defenses. Not even with his wife. So he battled her once again.

"I didn't tap into Nathan's wavelength because I didn't want to validate his lies. He lied about the budget! He lied on written reports! He lied to customers!"

"Settle down," said Cynthia. "No one is defending Nathan here."

"Sorry," said John Mark, rubbing his forehead.

He let out a lengthy sigh. "You're making an excellent point. Actually, you're teaching me something new. You're saying that to empathize is to track with a person's emotions, even if you disagree with what they're saying. Even if what they're saying is all wrong."

Cynthia responded, "To use your language, I suppose that I'm explaining what the Humanitarians' solution must be."

"But if you empathize with people, how do they ever change?" asked John Mark.

"They change in the same way as always," answered Cynthia. "They change from the inside out. People can change their behavior to an extent, but genuine transformation happens in the heart. True change is internal, don't you think?"

"Yes," said John Mark, pressing his back to the wall. "It's spiritual."

He paused for a second and then added, "I figure that since God sees the truth about who I am, I might as well face the truth myself."

John Mark raised his index finger, gesturing to his wife that he would be right back. Then he rushed downstairs to get the crumpled chart he'd been working on the night before.

"Your turn," he said. "What are your greatest strengths and weaknesses? And what are you trying to work on in your character?"

She put her elbows on her knees and rested her chin in her hands.

"As far as strengths," she began, "I'm high on compassion, empathy, kindness, patience, loyalty. I enjoy serving people and helping out. I appreciate good quality, but for me that usually means good quality service. I don't know what else. Is that enough?"

John Mark nodded.

"And your weaknesses?" he said gently.

"I'm very introspective; I'm always second-guessing myself, thinking that I should have done better.

"And I worry too much," she continued. "I care a lot about what other people think of me, and I wilt sometimes instead of speaking up when I ought to."

"What would you like to work on?" said John Mark.

"Becoming more principled in the way that I live," she answered. "I want to be more passionate about doing what is right and helping other people do what is right as well."

Then she clarified, "But I want to be diplomatic in the way that I do it."

"I've had the same thought," said John Mark.

"What are my next steps?" said Cynthia.

"Funny that you ask," said John Mark. "I made a little supplement to the People Model last night. It's an additional chart. I call it the Solutions Chart. The solutions illustrate how each type—at its best—deals with challenges.

"Let me show it to you. Okay, if you follow the chart *vertically*, you can apply whichever category you like. For instance, if you follow the Strategists' column, you can be bold to identify the problem, expose the problem, and fix the problem by speaking up and confronting the hard reality. When you do that, you stay true to sound ethics, which allows you to be real and unpretentious. After that, you provide evidence for your case if needed. Then you do your best to help everybody else focus on the facts as well.

"Or," he added, "you can apply all three columns at once. Theoretically, you can be bold and gracious and calm simultaneously."

He gave time for Cynthia to process.

"You could also do all three in sequence," John Mark said.

SOLUTIONS CHART

STRATEGIST Solutions	HUMANITARIAN Solutions	DIPLOMAT Solutions
Be Bold.	Be Gracious.	Be Calm.
Identify the Problem.	Empathize with Those Involved.	Put the Problem in Perspective.
Expose the Problem.	Help the Person/Team in Need.	Wait. / Be Sensitive to the Timing.
Fix the Problem.	Forbear the Problem.	Finesse the Problem.
Speak up. / Confront.	Listen. / Be Patient.	Preface & Nuance Your Remarks.
Be Ethical.	Be Supportive.	Be Creative.
Be Real. / Offer Evidence.	Be Kind. / Do a Favor.	Be Generous. / Give a Gift.
Focus on the Facts.	Focus on People's Feelings.	Focus on the Setting & Mood.

"Take the fourth line, for instance, and read it *horizontally* across the columns. At first you may choose to forbear a problem but later decide to fix it by finessing it somehow."

"This chart is so practical," said Cynthia. "It helps me to know better what to do."

"I like it," said John Mark, "because it specifies practical behaviors. You asked what I want to work on? I want to be more cognizant to put problems in perspective and to nuance my remarks by prefacing them, so that I don't inflame the people I'm trying to help."

"You're looking at the Diplomats' solutions," said Cynthia. "I like that column too. That last line in it tells me to pay attention to the setting I'm in."

"Yeah, I forget about that too," said John Mark. "My tendency is to think the facts can speak for themselves irrespective of location. But facts are understood in the context of a place. I have begun to learn that it's critically important to be mindful of *where* you are and *when* you decide to speak."

"Goodness, I'm overwhelmed again," said Cynthia. "I need to spend more time with this Solutions Chart. It's my favorite aspect of the People Model. Will it help me move away from people pleasing?"

"Yes," said John Mark, "because it guides you to help people instead of trying to please them."

"But overall," said Cynthia, "the Solutions Chart gives guidance for procedures; it does not address issues of the heart."

John Mark nodded. "That's right. But you can still create little exercises for yourself if you want to stop people pleasing so much. Want to hear a suggestion?" he asked.

"Definitely," said Cynthia.

"Picture in your mind the people you want to make happy."

Cynthia closed her eyes.

"Think of those you want to be 'in' with," said John Mark. "Those you're afraid to displease. Now concentrate on making a decision in advance *not* to be afraid of what those people think of you. Decide beforehand that you're going to be committed to their welfare no matter what, even if you have to challenge them."

"That's good advice," said Cynthia, "and yet I feel hesitant in a way."

"How come?" said John Mark.

"Because it feels so presumptuous for me to see myself as a catalyst to other people's growth. Who am I to challenge them? Besides, what if my judgment is wrong? And what if they don't even really *want* my help?"

"Listen to yourself, Cynthia!" he reproved. "The theme of your life is to help people! But all this murky thinking is now clouding your sense of purpose. You know that it's wrong to let a four-year-old ride his tricycle on the highway. On that you have clear thinking. Yet you wonder if it's okay to challenge grown-ups in the workplace who do things that are unethical or foolish. Cynthia, it's not good to let people cheat themselves out of living up to their potential. All of us do better when we challenge one another to be our best."

John Mark stopped short, thinking he might have been too forceful and alienated himself from his wife. But when he saw his wife's smile, it told him that the timing of his prodding had been just right. Rather than look offended, she seemed inspired.

CHAPTER 10

THREE FUNDAMENTAL TEMPTATIONS

The next weekend Cynthia found John Mark sitting on the porch studying his People Model chart. Before she had a chance to sit down, he began to share his latest musings.

"I landed on two other important insights," he announced.

"Wait a second, let me take a seat," she said, stroking his hair as she passed him.

John Mark leaned forward with his shoulders nearly hovering over his knees. "Here's the first one," he said. "If you lead from the upstairs, you're probably going to be criticized for doing so."

Cynthia looked puzzled.

"Let's start with the Strategists," he said. "They may seem like a threat just because they bring out the truth. The Humanitarians, in turn, may come across as weak just because they're patient and forbearing. The Diplomats, by contrast, may seem to be manipulative just because they're flexible and smooth."

Cynthia replied, "That actually makes sense because when Diplomats are in the basement, they truly *are* manipulative, and when Humanitarians are in the basement, they really *are* weak,

VIEWPOINT:	2nd Person (You) —Operational	3rd Person (He, She, They) —Cultural	1st Person (I, We) —Political
	STRATEGISTS (Light)	**HUMANITARIANS (Temp)**	**DIPLOMATS (Color)**
	Freedom	Compassion	Peace
	Authentic Community	Comfortable Community	Impressive Community
	Be Good	Feel Good	Look Good
	Clarity, Accountability	Develop, Support People	Sense of Harmony and Order
	Integrity	Togetherness	Unity
	Straightforward Message	Wise Approach	Wise Timing
	Confrontational, Spirited	Forbearing, Gentle	Nonconfrontational, Calm
	Discerning, Analytical	Patient, Kind	Finesse, Artful Demeanor
PERCEPTION:	*SEEMS THREATENING*	*SEEMS WEAK*	*SEEMS MANIPULATIVE*
	Corrective	Loyal	Polished, Refined
PRIORITY:	INFRASTRUCTURE	SERVICE	PUBLIC RELATIONS
	Self-Righteous	Self-Serving	Self-Absorbed
	Criticism, Harshness	People Pleasing	Image Management
	IS THREATENING	*IS WEAK*	*IS MANIPULATIVE*
BEHAVIOR:	Self-Righteous Judgment —Slander —Presumption —Impatience	Enablement —Gossip —Guilt Trips —Martyr Complex	Spin (Spin Club) —Distorts, Redefines Truth —Political Intimidation —Victim of Circumstances
THE PROBLEM:	PRIDE	FEAR	DECEITFULNESS

and when Strategists are in the basement, they actually *are* a threat."

John Mark reached for his copy of the chart.

"Excellent point," he said. "I didn't catch that before."

"The reason why *I* caught it," said Cynthia, "is because I'm afraid to come across as a threat to other people. I want people to perceive me as being supportive and approachable instead."

John Mark gently laughed. "I never thought about feeling afraid to be a threat. I get mad when people disregard the truth. Truth itself is what threatens them."

"I'm also afraid to come across as manipulative," said Cynthia. "I mean, I don't want to be perceived as being weak either, but if I am, it doesn't bother me that much."

"Hold it," said John Mark. "I want to point out something. It's *only* from the vantage point of the basement that upstairs behavior looks like downstairs behavior. Are you with me?"

"Sort of," said Cynthia.

He tried to slow down and explain, "Use your imagination and come stand with me in each basement for a second. Okay, from the perspective of the Strategists' basement, the Humanitarians seem spineless and weak, and the Diplomats seem deceptive and manipulative because the Strategist looks at them critically and judgmentally."

"Okay," said Cynthia, "now I see. And from the basement of the Humanitarians, the Diplomats can look like slick manipulators and the Strategists like dragon-breathing threats—because they're seen from the vantage point of fear."

John Mark added, "And from the basement of the Diplomats, the Strategists and the Humanitarians respectively seem threatening and weak—because the downstairs Diplomat mistakenly sees truth as an enemy and sacrificial giving as a waste of precious resources that could otherwise have been used to exalt the self."

"Very enlightening," said Cynthia. "What's the second thing you've thought of lately?"

John Mark became more enthused. "Remember I told you that I recently had a dream about Harvard?"

Cynthia nodded.

"I figured out why Harvard has been on my mind. I took this elective class there called 'Jesus and the Moral Life.' Basically the course challenged college students to find their moral bearings in a world that forces people to make hard decisions that none of our forebears faced. As our professor used to put it, 'We are trying to "do the right thing." . . . But what *is* "the right thing," and is Jesus any help in discerning it?'* The class was so popular that it attracted about seven hundred students every year: Jewish people, Muslims, atheists, Buddhists, law students, science majors, philosophy majors, Catholics, and Protestants like me."

As John Mark recounted the story, his face lit up.

"Though I certainly disagreed with the professor at times, he always got me thinkng. For instance, I remember him telling us that Jesus of Nazareth was a rabbi. I thought that was funny at the time. Having been raised by Methodist parents, it cracked me up to realize that Jesus wasn't a Christian—he was a Jewish rabbi.

"Well anyway," he said, "I started thinking about that class and dug out my notes the other day. One session was on how the devil tempted Jesus in the wilderness three times. When I read what I'd written in class, it hit me. . . ."

John Mark's face became brighter.

"Cynthia," he stated, "you won't believe how those temptations relate to business. And they totally reflect the People Model."

"I'm not sure I can remember all three of them," she said. "Let's see—"

John Mark was so excited that he cut in. "The temptations were to jump off the pinnacle of the Temple, turn the stones into bread, and bow down and worship Satan."

"That doesn't sound like business talk," said Cynthia. "But it does seem to line up with the People Model, at least in part."

John Mark ceded the conversation to his wife. He was eager to find out if she could discern how the three temptations correlate with everyday life.

Cynthia asserted, "When Satan tempted Jesus to throw himself off the Temple, he was tempting Jesus to show off. He was trying to get Jesus to summon a group of angels and prove that he was God. That's the temptation in the Diplomats' column," she said.

"Yes," said John Mark. "All of us are tempted to glorify ourselves. We all want people to admire us. And truth be told, we want to take more credit than we deserve."

"I see," said Cynthia. "Jesus was a miracle worker but not a show-off. No wonder people worship him. That's remarkable."

"It is," said John Mark. "Yet I'm even more amazed by his resistance to turn the dry stones into bread."

"On that one," said Cynthia, "the temptation was for Jesus to break his fast. He hadn't eaten anything in three or four weeks, right?"

"Almost six weeks," said John Mark.

"Wow," said Cynthia.

"In the desert," John Mark added. "Jesus was in the desert all by himself with no food. It must have been so tempting to succumb to the devil's order and turn the dry stones into bread."

"I have no idea how this relates to the People Model, much less to the business community," said Cynthia.

John Mark responded, "I never made the connection myself until I remembered that we talked about this in class. On one level, the devil was tempting Jesus to break his fast prematurely. But on a deeper level, he was tempting him to be an impatient fixer. The devil was tempting Jesus to take control of the results. To rebel against unresolve. To be too prideful to endure the humbling pain of having stones instead of bread."

"That's fascinating," said Cynthia.

"It's convicting," said John Mark. "The core temptation in the Strategists' category is to oversimplify complicated things. To go for the pat answer, the presumption. To be intolerant of mystery and ambiguity. To be too immature to withstand the sight of something unexplained or unfixed or unresolved.

"If you think about it, Jesus could have fixed the situation," said John Mark. "He could've turned the rocks into bread. But he was humble enough to wait. Humble enough to trust God when the problem of having no food still wasn't fixed."

"I never would've figured that out," said Cynthia. "I can't figure out the last one either. If this is the temptation of the Humanitarians' column, I don't even begin to be able to see it. Satan urged Jesus to bow down and worship him in exchange for inheriting the world. That has nothing at all to do with people pleasing."

"This temptation," said John Mark, "is very subtle. Therefore, it is very seductive.

"Anytime a person is tempted to bow down to the status quo—in other words, anytime a person buys into the lie that 'there is really nothing I can do about it'—that, my dear, is the equivalent of bowing down to Satan.

"If you're trying to picture this," John Mark went on to say, "then you have to understand that Jesus wasn't being tempted to kiss the feet of a little red imp. There wasn't any pitchfork or horns or anything cartoonlike about it. Jesus was being tempted to be complicit. The temptation was for him not to die for the world, but rather to let it persist in its unredeemed state. The devil wanted Jesus to give in to inertia. To follow the path of least resistance. The fundamental temptation in the Humanitarians' column is to bow down to the excuse that 'we've got too much momentum to make a change' or that 'it's always been done this way; therefore, no one has the right or power to stop it.'"

Cynthia took his statement and personalized it. "You're telling me that refusing to blow the whistle is tantamount to bowing down to Satan?!"

"It's a root pressure, isn't it?"

"Bowing down to Satan is way worse than keeping your mouth shut when other people are doing wrong," Cynthia argued. She sounded too defensive to John Mark.

He responded unemotionally, "When people allow evil to have its way, the devil wins. Can't you see? It puts the devil in charge."

Cynthia got up, marched into the house, locked herself in the bedroom, and iced her husband out. After seeing his wife's reaction, John Mark's prideful anger heated up. The contrast between the two of them was stunning.

He followed her into the house and yelled into the air, "See what I mean?! The Strategist seems like a threat whenever someone else is in the basement!"

Three hours later, John Mark realized what had happened. Both he and his wife had dropped into the basement and indulged the very temptations that Jesus had resisted.

Unlike John Mark, who was yelling at his wife and trying to

control her behavior, Jesus had refused to fix the dry stones by turning them into bread. And unlike Cynthia, who was wallowing in guilt and self-pity, Jesus didn't cling to the status quo. Whereas Cynthia felt defeated by her paralyzing fear, Jesus had the courage to be triumphant.

After thinking it through, John Mark walked upstairs to apologize to his wife.

*Harvey Cox, *When Jesus Came to Harvard* (New York: Houghton Mifflin, 2004), 21. Cox wrote and taught the course "Jesus and the Moral Life" for about twenty years at Harvard. Please note that I have tweaked his insights on Jesus' temptations to fit my own convictions, as voiced by the character John Mark.

CHAPTER 11

THREE KINDS
OF POWER

Two months later, John Mark and Lisa were scheduled for a meeting, and if ever the time was ripe for a momentous conversation, it was now. Lisa was about to begin a special project with the president, and the stakes of the deal were high. If they could manage to cinch it, the company would secure a record profit.

He greeted her at the coffeehouse where the two of them usually met.

"How are you?" he asked.

"I'm swamped," said Lisa.

"Yeah, I hear that you're about to be involved in some very special meetings with the president."

"You've got that right," said Lisa.

"Have you thought about the timing of all this?" asked John Mark.

"The timing of all what?"

"The timing of your meetings."

"What do you mean?"

"It's providential," John Mark said plainly. "The timing is providential. You've got the perfect opportunity to talk to Max."

Lisa seemed unmoved.

"Lisa," said John Mark, trying his best to convince her. "You know that Nathan is disloyal to the president. He's won the sympathy of many by giving them the impression that the president removed him because Max felt intolerably upstaged. A growing number of people actually believe that Max couldn't handle supervising someone of Nathan's caliber."

Lisa's countenance began to change. She appeared to be a bit tense.

John Mark spoke again. "Don't be surprised if Max suddenly decides to remove you from his circle."

"What are you talking about?" said Lisa incredulously.

"Nathan may not want you around," said John Mark. "Remember what I said about divide and conquer? If I know Nathan, what he will try to do is play on Max's fear. Nathan will create the perception that you're the wrong person to be in Max's inner circle. He'll attempt to convince Max that the stakes are too high to take a chance on keeping you around."

"I thought you said that Nathan was all bluff," responded Lisa.

"He is," said John Mark. "But people buy into his spin."

Lisa bristled. "Why drop this in my lap again?" she said.

"Because it's already in your lap," John Mark stated. "Providentially, you're the one who can walk through the front door and tell the CEO what he doesn't want to hear but what he *needs* to hear."

"I'm the president's subordinate," she said. "Who am I to presume to be his adviser?"

"You're hired to be a special consultant," John Mark stated. "He's paying you to give him your best advice."

"But he wants my advice on an outside deal, not an inside personnel problem."

"The two are inseparable," said John Mark.

"You're asking me to risk getting fired," Lisa declared. "Max will be insulted if I go in there and try to tell him what to do."

"But if you say nothing, and Max joins Nathan's spin club, then Nathan will attempt to squeeze you out. After that, I wouldn't be surprised if he subtly finds a way to shift the blame on Max for the shortfall in the budget that Nathan himself created some months ago. I don't know how he'll do it, but if I know Nathan, he'll try to pull it off in desperation."

John Mark added, "It's all a matter of timing. Whoever reaches Max first—you or Nathan—that's who I predict will win the day."

"You actually think Nathan would try to push me out?" she asked.

John Mark shrugged. "He did it to me, didn't he?

"And if things go awry," John Mark added, "you will have to live with yourself, knowing that you—of all people—had a special opportunity to be the unseen hero of the company."

"Fired if it goes wrong, and unseen if it goes right," Lisa said. "That's really motivating for me."

"This is your moment," John Mark said. "You've got all the right skills to succeed. The question is whether or not you have the character."

"So what do you propose that I do?" she asked.

"I propose that you use your creativity and vision, and figure out the answer yourself."

"I'm not like you, John Mark."

"That's good," said John Mark. "You have a better chance of succeeding than I did."

"What makes you say that?" said Lisa.

"You're more naturally a Diplomat. I wasn't diplomatic enough."

"Yeah, but unlike the rest of us, you kept your integrity," she said.

John Mark didn't highlight her confession—"unlike the rest of us." He was learning not to be so confrontational.

"I'm less of a Strategist than you are," she said, "and I appreciate my job. Besides, someday I would like to lead a company myself. Being fired is not going to lift me to the top."

"You have to decide what kind of leader—what kind of person—you want to become," John Mark challenged. "This is a turning point, both for you and the company."

"I wish you wouldn't put it like that," Lisa said. "Life would be easier if you would lighten up here and there."

"Life would be easier," he said, "if there weren't any battles to fight. Leadership above the line is all about doing the right thing. Doing the right thing instead of slouching in the basement and choosing your own thing at the expense of everyone else."

"What *is* the right thing?" Lisa asked.

"The right thing is to fight the good fight by standing in the truth. It is to prioritize people by taking calculated risks on their behalf. The right thing is to establish peace by uniting what is true with what is good."

"You sound like Superman, John Mark."

John Mark tried to be calm. "Let me clarify," he said. "If you fight the wrong fight, you're simply wasting time being quarrelsome and petty. And if you don't fight at all, then the forces of destruction take over."

"What you're saying sounds so abstract," said Lisa. "I have to live in the real world."

John Mark deflected her remark by refusing to absorb it or correct it. "I'm talking about leadership," he said. "And leadership is leadership, whether you're a special consultant to the president—or someday the president yourself. The principles of leadership are the same. In every case, first-rate leaders exercise good character. To be a great leader is to be a great person. In other words, you can't develop patterns of doing the right thing unless you become the right person."

"But you have to admit, don't you, that sometimes great leaders lead ignoble causes? Hitler was effective, wasn't he?" said Lisa.

"I wouldn't call Hitler a leader. Hitler was a *misleader.* People weren't led by him; they were *misled* by him. Hitler operated from the basement. To be a first-rate leader is to lead from the upstairs—above the line."

"Name one person who does this all the time," challenged Lisa.

"Jesus did it," said John Mark.

"You think Jesus was a Strategist?" Lisa asked.

"Why do you think they killed him?" John Mark answered.

"See? You just said it," she argued. "I'll get fired if I try to talk to Max."

"But Jesus was a Diplomat too," said John Mark. "He finessed his way out of politically loaded situations time and time again. You'd be inspired to find out how clever he was.

"He also was a Humanitarian," John Mark added. "A man of service and action. He was constantly on the move—healing people, serving people, and reaching out to his friends. It's not as though the Cross was the only episode of Jesus' life."

"But the Cross is what made him famous," Lisa said.

"No, what made him famous is that he rose from the dead," John Mark answered. "Jesus conquered death by entering death. He miraculously blasted through it by rising from it three days after he died. That's why I believe he can transform people's character."

"Well, that's fine for you," said Lisa. "But the story of Jesus is so far removed from the reality of our company that it almost seems irrelevant to be talking about him."

"The choice is yours," said John Mark. "There is no obligation, just an opportunity. You can either do the right thing or not."

"How can you be sure that you know what the right thing is?" Lisa countered.

"If you were Max, would you want to be told or not?"

"Max is a very capable person. I believe he'll do all right without my help."

"And how will the company fare?" said John Mark. "And what if you've been placed here at this particular time for this particular task? What if you're that vital and important to the future of the company?"

John Mark could see that his words were penetrating, so he went on. "Can I tell you what I've learned just recently?" For the next several minutes, he explained to Lisa what he had remembered from his class at Harvard.

"Lisa, I want you to gain from the People Model just as much as I have," he added. "It's all so clear to me now. The People Model yields three different kinds of power: *explanatory power, motivational power,* and *creative power.*"

He reached into his briefcase and spread out his latest copy of the People Model.

Then he explained the explanatory power of the model. That

is, he showed her how the model *anticipates* the relational dynamics that actually play out in real life.

When he finished, Lisa said, "Oh, I see. The People Model

	Explanatory Power	Motivational Power	Creative Power
VIEWPOINT:	2nd Person (You) —Operational	3rd Person (He, She, They) —Cultural	1st Person (I, We) —Political
	STRATEGISTS (Light)	**HUMANITARIANS** (Temp)	**DIPLOMATS** (Color)
	Freedom	Compassion	Peace
	Authentic Community	Comfortable Community	Impressive Community
	Be Good	Feel Good	Look Good
	Clarity, Accountability	Develop, Support People	Sense of Harmony and Order
	Integrity	Togetherness	Unity
	Straightforward Message	Wise Approach	Wise Timing
	Confrontational, Spirited	Forbearing, Gentle	Nonconfrontational, Calm
	Discerning, Analytical	Patient, Kind	Finesse, Artful Demeanor
PERCEPTION:	SEEMS THREATENING	SEEMS WEAK	SEEMS MANIPULATIVE
	Corrective	Loyal	Polished, Refined
PRIORITY:	INFRASTRUCTURE	SERVICE	PUBLIC RELATIONS
	Self-Righteous	Self-Serving	Self-Absorbed
	Criticism, Harshness	People Pleasing	Image Management
	IS THREATENING	IS WEAK	IS MANIPULATIVE
BEHAVIOR:	Self-Righteous Judgment —Slander —Presumption —Impatience	Enablement —Gossip —Guilt Trips —Martyr Complex	Spin (Spin Club) —Distorts, Redefines Truth —Political Intimidation —Victim of Circumstances
THE PROBLEM:	PRIDE	FEAR	DECEITFULNESS

predicts that a below-the-line Diplomat will usually dominate a below-the-line Humanitarian."

"Yes," said John Mark. "It's relatively easy for a basement Diplomat to intimidate a basement Humanitarian because Humanitarians in the basement already feel afraid, though often their fear is subconscious."

"I see," said Lisa. "So when Nathan fell into the basement, he held an advantage over Max because Max enabled him."

"Right," said John Mark. "In fact, the People Model offers an alternative perspective as well. It shows what *could* have happened instead. If Max would have sidestepped into the Strategist category and remained *above the line*, the People Model suggests that the opposite result would've happened. Max would have held the advantage over Nathan. In other words, Max could have called Nathan's bluff."

Reflecting further, John Mark added, "Of course, Nathan would have still had his connections, and he still could have toyed with the politics."

"Especially with those board members," Lisa said, agreeing with John Mark.

"Even so," John Mark continued, "Max could have undermined Nathan's credibility by preventing him from speaking as an insider. Any fallout for Max probably would have been short-term, because the only people who were likely to keep siding with Nathan were those who weren't informed enough to see through Nathan's gimmicky ways of speaking."

John Mark then concluded, "So, if Max would have spent time with the top two or three of Nathan's sympathizers, he might have been able to turn the situation around by exposing them to the hard facts. If that proved not to work, then at least he would have learned who to eliminate or who to build more trust with."

Lisa responded, "But if Max had talked with those who defended Nathan, he and Nathan might have had a falling out."

John Mark was trying hard not to judge her. To him, it seemed plain that Lisa was worrying about herself—worrying about her own rapport with Max.

"Do you see what I mean?" said Lisa.

Because John Mark was still being overly presumptuous in that moment, he was blind to the validity of Lisa's point. Defaulting to the Strategists' basement, he said impatiently, "The point is, Max is worried about himself. Obviously he feels guilty about having promoted Nathan in the first place. It's also pretty clear that Max is busy protecting his own image. Let's put it out in the open—for Max to fire Nathan is for him to tell the company that he, as the president, failed."

"But isn't it also plausible that Max prefers not to have a falling out with Nathan?" said Lisa.

"Well, of course," said John Mark, "but the primary point still remains."

Still trying to make sense of why Max had publicly praised Nathan, Lisa asked, "But why did Max praise Nathan right after he had removed him from the executive team?"

"If you look back at the chart, the People Model tells you that Max probably felt intimidated by the pressure he was getting from Nathan's spin club."

Lisa nodded.

Continuing, he explained, "If Nathan let it leak that he was victimized by jealousy, then Max probably caught some flack from Nathan's spin club."

Lisa took a moment to weigh his answer.

"So then what did Max do in response to the pressure from Nathan's spin club?" said John Mark.

"He praised Nathan publicly," she said.

"Why?"

"To attempt to quell the ire of Nathan's defenders?" Lisa guessed. "To make himself look amicable and appreciative rather than jealous?"

"Those are good guesses," said John Mark. "And what was the grand effect of that move?"

"It backfired," Lisa said.

She had noticed this before, but she didn't have the language to describe it. Thanks to the People Model, now she understood that Max's public praises were lending credibility to Nathan's victim story and causing Nathan's spin club to grow. In other words, Max's spin made Nathan's spin seem truthful.

John Mark went on, "It certainly is no secret that Max wants the company to grow exponentially. In almost every speech, he talks about growth and expansion. Rarely does he talk about quality."

"He talks about quality to the customers," Lisa said.

"That's different. I'm referring to the fact that he leads around the concept of expansion. His business decisions reveal what he cares about most. He wants us to be large, not great."

"I'm not so sure about that," said Lisa.

"Well, I can tell you this," said John Mark. "The less the CEO prioritizes quality, the more risky it becomes for anyone to bring out the truth."

"That's why I'm hesitant to speak," said Lisa.

John Mark could tell that Lisa didn't realize she had revealed her honest convictions once again. To calm himself, he cleared his throat. He wanted so much to confront her, but he knew that indicting her would cause her to delay. He wanted to be a catalyst, not a deterrent.

Successfully having restrained himself, he added, "And when enough people quit caring about quality, then the company starts scapegoating the Strategists whenever they raise the banner of authenticity—because they will surely seem like a threat."

"That's what happened to you," she said. "You were scapegoated."

"Scapegoated, yes, but only by Nathan, not Max."

From the look on Lisa's face, John Mark could tell that Lisa felt conflicted inside.

John Mark added, "From Max's perspective, Nathan probably seemed like an answer to prayer. He could talk big without worrying about the restraints of reality. I firmly believe people bought into him because he lavishly spent money on things that made his words seem credible. He drove the right car, wore the right clothes, dropped the right names, used the right buzzwords, and delegated his work so that he would be freed to manage his persona full-time."

"So if the president was a little bit afraid," said Lisa, "and a little bit affected by the glamour of his own position, then he might have taken security in Nathan's sense of calm and self-assurance, and he might have felt esteemed by Nathan's lofty plan to build a vast empire of alliances."

"Right on," said John Mark. "That is why in times like these it's imperative for Diplomats and Humanitarians to sidestep into the upstairs of the Strategists' category and for Strategists to rise out of the basement. Yessiree, it takes a critical mass of people to recapture the integrity of a company."

"I believe in Max," said Lisa. "I think he wants to do the right thing."

"Then exercise your faith in him by calling him to rise above the line. Give him the opportunity to respond to your best advice."

"But how do I get myself into the upstairs of the Strategists' category so that I can be bold and confrontational?" Lisa asked.

"You tell me," said John Mark.

"By valuing truth," she said.

"And by valuing your own character," John Mark added. "If you really want to be a first-rate leader, then make it your goal to stay above the line in all three categories."

"That's challenging," Lisa said.

"And motivating," said John Mark. "The motivational power of the People Model is that it helps you to *believe* that you don't need the basement anymore. Lisa, you don't have to take security in your persona in order to be a persuasive Diplomat. You can afford to be faithful to your conscience."

"A lot of people in business really don't have a conscience," she replied. "They'll do anything in order to make it big."

"So?"

"So, if I become this predictable Strategist, then other Diplomats will have an advantage over me because when they magnify themselves and appear to be bigger than life, I'll come across as plain Jane bound by old-fashioned principles."

"Lisa, tell me what's predictable about good principles and truth. Just because a person predictably honors a code of ethics and tells the truth doesn't mean that her business decisions are predictable! Telling the truth is like cooperating with reality, and reality is always changing, even though some elements remain the same. Dealing truthfully with reality is a strategic thing to do, and it hardly gives away a leader's hand."

"In reality," said Lisa, "the good guy doesn't always win. You know as well as I do that you can have a great business strategy and still lose out if your competitor looks better to the public than you do. Sometimes perceptions matter more than reality. To me, it's very important to manage public perceptions carefully."

Lisa was talking about herself, not the company.

John Mark responded gently, "If people perceive that you're an honest person, Lisa, will that make you honest inside? If people perceive that you're happy and at peace with yourself, will that give you inner fulfillment?"

He looked her right in the eye.

"I'm trying to help you," he said.

"And I'm trying to help Max," said Lisa in a cavalier tone.

"Help Max do what?" said John Mark, refusing to give up on Lisa's character. "Maintain his false perception of Nathan? Help Max stay in the dark about the truth of what's really happening? Who are you really helping, Lisa?"

"What if your analysis is mistaken?" she said.

"My analysis is irrelevant," said John Mark. "The ball is in your court, not mine."

"Well, then let's talk about the third power now," she said. "You know, the creative power of the People Model. I know that it pertains to figuring out what to do with all the information the People Model provides."

"According to the People Model," said John Mark, "it's best to employ a wise approach when confronting a Humanitarian such as Max."

Lisa pressed, "But how are you supposed to know what a wise approach is?"

"Good question," said John Mark. "Tell me what the answer is. Tell me what the Solutions Chart suggests."

Lisa stalled by stirring a Sweet'n Low in her coffee and taking another sip of her drink.

"A wise approach," she began intrepidly, "means to follow the

SOLUTIONS CHART

STRATEGIST Solutions	HUMANITARIAN Solutions	DIPLOMAT Solutions
Be Bold.	Be Gracious.	Be Calm.
Identify the Problem.	Empathize with Those Involved.	Put the Problem in Perspective.
Expose the Problem.	Help the Person/Team in Need.	Wait. / Be Sensitive to the Timing.
Fix the Problem.	Forbear the Problem.	Finesse the Problem.
Speak up. / Confront.	Listen. / Be Patient.	Preface & Nuance Your Remarks.
Be Ethical.	Be Supportive.	Be Creative.
Be Real. / Offer Evidence.	Be Kind. / Do a Favor.	Be Generous. / Give a Gift.
Focus on the Facts.	Focus on People's Feelings.	Focus on the Setting & Mood.

Solutions Chart of the Humanitarians. It means to be gracious and gentle. It means that I go there for the purpose of helping Max in his need. It also means to focus on Max's feelings."

"That's right," said John Mark. "So how can you approach him and say the hard thing that needs to be said in this case?"

Lisa's eyes widened.

"I get it," she said, smiling at John Mark. "Since Max is primarily a Humanitarian, it's best to begin by taking time at first to value Max. A wise approach would entail expressing appreciation for him, telling him again that I believe in him as a leader and encouraging him with honest affirmations."

"Anything else?" said John Mark.

"Well, there must be something else since you said that," said Lisa. She couldn't help but grin because she knew John Mark was coaching her for success.

"I would need to be careful about the timing," she added. "I'd have to talk to Max in private when he's ready to hear the truth. It would certainly be unwise to talk to him in public, even on the sidelines where no one else can hear the conversation. And it would also be unwise to confront him when he's feeling presidential because then he might be more sensitive to criticism."

John Mark nodded, but then looked at her as if to say that she had left something out.

"What?" said Lisa, not knowing what else to say.

"Eventually you have to be bold," said John Mark. "Eventually you have to be straightforward enough for him to understand exactly what you want him to hear."

"Yes, that would be important," she said.

CHAPTER 12

LEADING
ABOVE THE LINE

The next week Lisa phoned John Mark. He was reading files in his office.

"I can't go through with it. I can't put my job on the line."

"Is that what you're telling yourself?" he responded.

"John Mark, it's not enough to *know* what the right thing is. Just because I know that eating fried foods is unhealthy doesn't mean that I can automatically cut them out of my diet."

"You've learned that," said John Mark.

"No one is perfect," Lisa said. "So we're all going to have to live with our imperfections."

"Does that mean you're giving up?"

"I'm a Diplomat, not a Strategist," she said.

"I thought you wanted to become a first-rate leader."

"It might be more realistic for me to strive to become a first-rate Diplomat."

"A first-rate Diplomat who doesn't trust her boss?" said John Mark.

"All along I've told you that I believe in Max," Lisa argued.

John Mark answered, "But you think Max will fire you if you offer him a chance to reevaluate his decision regarding Nathan?"

"I wish I could visit with you more," she said, "but I've got a lot of work in front of me. I'll catch you later."

She hung up the phone only to find an urgent e-mail from Max's secretary.

> Lisa,
> Max can't make your afternoon meeting today. An emergency came up with Nathan Gorman regarding the client. I'll get back to you to reschedule.
> On behalf of Max

Suddenly Lisa's heart began to pound.

Meanwhile John Mark went back to reading his files. In the process he came across an old memo that Nathan had sent him about a month before demoting John Mark. He couldn't help but read it again.

The memo was typical—too complimentary and amorphous—and, of course, sent indirectly through Nathan's secretary. It said:

> John Mark:
> Wanted to express my appreciation for your fine contribution to the company during these days of constant change and

cultural turbulence. Good managers can be difficult to find, especially ones like you who understand the difference between leadership and management. I want to be very careful in the days ahead to strive to maximize your potential and to identify new ways to utilize your input on strategic matters that pertain to your level of management.

NG

Executive Vice President

For Nathan to have sent it had raised a red flag in John Mark's mind. Looking at it now, it seemed more like a gesture than a memo. A gesture. A power play, that is. A little written reminder that Nathan saw himself as a leader and John Mark as a manager working under him. It also hinted at Nathan's desire to be unchallenged by John Mark on strategic matters ("I want to be very careful . . . to identify new ways to utilize your input on strategic matters.") New ways. Ways that didn't challenge Nathan's ideas.

John Mark was convinced that what had nagged at Nathan most was his lack of fear. Nathan never could find a hook by which to make John Mark believe that Nathan was superior to him.

Conversely, what had irked John Mark the most were Nathan's pompous statements that were always off the record and hard to quote. Nathan knew the art of saying "Blah, blah, blah" in fancy language. His habit was to utter very patronizing things about the president. He maneuvered politically by calculating ways to transfer people's confidence away from Max and to himself. But then, as a matter of routine, the tables would completely turn around. In the presence of Max, Nathan would express undying loyalty.

Exactly what Max thought was hard to tell. It was clear Max

knew there was a problem. After all, he did remove Nathan from the number two seat. But since he didn't remove Nathan from the company, John Mark was still convinced that something deep in Max was unresolved.

John Mark began thinking of King David in Jewish history, the king who enabled Absalom, his Diplomat son. Absalom was a political usurper. Nevertheless, King David gave him enough latitude to cause a civil war within the kingdom. As King David had enabled his son Absalom, so Max was still enabling Nathan Gorman. Even now, Nathan was drawing a considerable full-time salary—though his job did not entail a full-time load.

Like it or not, Nathan had a gift for managing up. He could always find a way to make Max feel heroic. Specifically, it seemed to John Mark that Nathan's stately manner, his quickness on his feet, his poise, his self-confidence—combined with his dependence on Max—made Nathan a walking symbol of what it meant to make Max feel important. So the two of them bonded in a symbiotic way with Max as the boss and Nathan as the subordinate who carried himself as the king. Nathan would create new alliances, and Max would bestow rich favor on him as a result. The challenge for Nathan was to manage the balancing act of presenting himself as king to the new alliances and giving Max the royal treatment back at headquarters.

That same evening, just as John Mark was about to turn out the light and go to sleep, he said to Cynthia, "What's it going to take to wake up Max? And what's it going to take to motivate Lisa?"

Cynthia answered with a question, "Do you think you're trying to fix them?"

"I'm just wondering if they'll *ever* get fixed," he replied.

"Are you feeling discouraged?" she asked.

"No. I'm being impatient," he said. "I'm sorry."

Cynthia suggested, "Why don't you try to empathize with Lisa? Try to stand in her shoes for a second. Then try to empathize with Max."

"Empathy," said John Mark. "Empathy is the antidote to impatience."

"I wouldn't want to be in Lisa's position," said Cynthia. "She's worked so hard and come so far, especially when you compare her to other women. Lisa is making it. So far she's winning the game. For her to risk her status at this point in her career almost seems reckless. Give her a few more years of experience and she'll probably be on her way to becoming a CEO of another company. When you think about it, the last thing Lisa needs is a setback."

"But if she doesn't make the hard decision," said John Mark, "then she won't be as effective of an executive leader later. She may get there, but she'll be impoverished internally unless she cultivates her character along the way."

"Yes, but can you appreciate the challenge she is facing? Can you bring yourself to be more of a cheerleader to her rather than a critical coach?"

"I give Lisa encouragement," said John Mark.

"I'm talking about giving her your faith," said Cynthia. "Believing in her more. Cheering her on. Applauding in the grandstands as she tries to run the race."

"That's what you want me to do for you as well," said John Mark. He sighed.

"I'm working on it," he said. "What you're saying is right, and I want you to feel my support. And I want to be a good support to Lisa."

"Lisa is relying on the strengths that have promoted her so

far," Cynthia added. "The real risk for her is to learn how to lean on an additional set of strengths—Strategist strengths."

"Your point is well taken," said John Mark. "In this situation, it feels awkward for Lisa to be primarily a Strategist and awkward for me to be primarily a Diplomat."

"Now you're getting the message," said Cynthia.

"Yes," said John Mark, "this is Lisa's opportunity—a golden opportunity—to come to grips with who she is."

"What do you mean?"

"This situation is a litmus test," said John Mark. "It's time for her to find out if Lisa—the real Lisa—can make it as a leader. As long as Lisa values her image over herself, then she will have to lead from an artificial place, and she will always carry an inner emptiness.

"But you want to know something?" he added. "I have a sense that there's another obstacle provoking Lisa's unwillingness to go forward. I think Lisa is resistant because she's the kind of person who won't want to be a hypocrite for long. Before she confronts Max, she'll confront herself. That's what she's resistant to—confronting herself."

"You've really thought about this, haven't you?" said Cynthia. "You believe in her, don't you?"

"I'd like to," said John Mark, "but she might not turn around."

"Has the People Model helped her?" Cynthia asked.

"Perhaps," said John Mark, "and yet the People Model has no inherent power. It's like every other tool. A hammer is totally useless unless someone picks it up."

"That's true," said Cynthia. "The People Model can't change anyone by itself."

"People can't change themselves all by themselves," said John Mark. "We have to look beyond ourselves to change."

"What I've noticed about myself," said Cynthia, "is that my behavior tends to conform to whomever I'm trying to please. I wish it weren't true, but I can be such a chameleon."

"It's easy to be a chameleon," said John Mark, "because chameleonlike behavior is acceptable to the crowd."

"That's exactly my point," said Cynthia. "Chameleons look more innocent than they are."

"Has the People Model helped you to understand that?"

"Yes, by all means."

"So we're back to the same point," said John Mark. "To be changed from the inside out requires genuine transformation."

Cynthia responded, "I think I need God's help for that to happen."

"There's really no other way," agreed John Mark. "Unless you look to God for help, your heart won't change. But if you have the right heart, other things will fall into place."

"I agree," said Cynthia. "To *lead* above the line is to *live* above the line."

They looked at the clock and realized that they needed to get some sleep.

The next day John Mark received a call from Max's secretary. She said the president wanted to see him right away.

John Mark had no idea what the meeting might be about. The only thing he could think of was that Max might want to discuss some decisions that the new vice president of sales had made. From what John Mark had heard, the rest of the sales team was unhappy about the changes he was making.

"Hello, Max," said John Mark. The two of them shook hands.

"Have a seat," said the president. "I want to talk to you about something important. I've been studying the records around here. In the course of my study, it has come to my attention that you have been more faithful to honor the budget and more fruitful in your sales than anyone else in the company. You have also done a great job of adjusting to the field once again. On top of all that, you have quite an impressive past as a supervisor in internal operations."

Within minutes John Mark had agreed to become the new executive vice president.

As soon as he got back to his office, Lisa knocked on the door.

"I have some news for you," she said with great enthusiasm.

"You already know?" said John Mark. "That's odd, because I just found out myself."

"So what do you say?"

"I say that I've got a lot of work ahead of me," he replied.

"What do you mean?" she said. "I thought you'd cheer."

"I haven't had time to process. But overall, it does feel good. In fact, before you walked in, I was about to call Cynthia."

"It's amazing, isn't it? I didn't get fired after all!"

"What?" said John Mark. "I thought you were talking about my promotion."

"Your promotion? You got promoted?"

"Yeah, I was just named the new executive vice president. But it won't be announced for another two weeks."

"John Mark, that's awesome! Congratulations!"

"So you went in and talked to Max after all?"

"Yeah, my big news is that Max fired Nathan yesterday."

"What did you say to Max?"

"To begin with, I told him that I honestly couldn't imagine

having a president more loyal and committed to the company. Then I expressed my appreciation and told him that I believe in him as a leader," she explained.

"Then what did you do?" asked John Mark.

"I showed him the People Model."

"You what?"

"I spent a full hour explaining it. I didn't tell him all of it. I just gave him the bare bones of the model.

"What's most incredible," she added, "is that after I explained the People Model and Max mulled over it for a few minutes, he looked at me and said, 'I never saw this before.' 'Saw what?' I asked.

"He said, 'I never saw before how protective John Mark is of the company's integrity. You know, sometimes John Mark can seem too strict, but he's certainly a straight shooter—very, very different from Nathan.'"

John Mark could hardly believe his ears.

"That's when I stuck out my neck," said Lisa. "The moment was ripe, and I knew it."

"So what'd you say next?" said John Mark.

"I asked him which category he thought Nathan was in when he moved you down from being VP."

John Mark was dumbstruck.

"Suddenly Max got fiery," said Lisa. "I've never seen him get that way before. He slid his finger down the chart in the Diplomat column. Then he started shaking his head. That's when he asked me a question."

"What?" said John Mark. "What'd he ask you?"

"He asked if I trust Nathan."

"And what'd you say to that?"

"I said, 'Trust him in what way?'"

"You had the wherewithal to ask a clarifying question in that intense of a moment?! Lisa, you amaze me!"

Lisa got a cool look on her face and calmly grinned.

"Well, c'mon! Get on with the story!" urged John Mark.

"Then Max said to me, 'Do you think Nathan's loyal to the company?' And I answered, 'I think he'd be very loyal—at least in his own way—if he were the president of the company.' Then Max said, 'The president of the company?' And I just nodded my head as soberly as I could. That's when Max slammed his hand down on the table."

"Do you think Max understood that his leadership style had been allowing Nathan to plot against him?"

"He understood something," said Lisa. "He was furious."

"I bet Max's blind spot wasn't even on Nathan. It must've been on himself. Until you talked with him, I bet he didn't see how he'd been enabling Nathan. I betcha that's what it was."

John Mark let out a sigh and said, "Lisa, you're brilliant."

"The People Model did it," she answered. "I think the People Model helped Max see how destructive it is for a Humanitarian in the basement to sponsor a Diplomat in the basement."

John Mark cheered. "It worked! The People Model worked!"

"It worked beautifully," said Lisa.

"Wise approach," said John Mark. "Max is a Humanitarian, and you used a wise approach with him."

"Timing," she countered. "It was a matter of timing."

"And finesse," said John Mark. "That was awesome."

"I have a great coach," said Lisa. She motioned with her hand as if to tip her hat to John Mark.

"But wait, you've got to tell me," he said. "When did you decide to go in and speak to Max? You had even phoned to tell me that you weren't going to bring it up to him."

"I know," Lisa said. "But after getting an e-mail from Max's secretary, I realized you were right. Everything you had warned me of vividly came to mind."

"So how did you find time to meet with Max?"

"I persuaded Max's secretary to let me talk to him right away. It had come to my attention that he was supposed to meet with Nathan and the client."

"In hearing you tell the story, I can only imagine the suspense," said John Mark.

"Oh," said Lisa, "my heart was pounding until I stepped into Max's office. I can't tell you how relieved I was to talk to him in time."

John Mark chuckled empathetically.

"Wait a minute," he said, shifting thoughts. "How did you find out that Max fired Nathan?"

"Nathan's secretary called my secretary."

"What an incredible turn of events," said John Mark. "You'd think the whole story came right out of the book of Esther in the Bible."

"I don't know the story. Fill me in."

"It only roughly parallels," John Mark said. "Basically, the story is about a Jewish woman who risked her life by doing the right thing. She was sort of like you, Lisa, except that Esther was the queen in Persia long, long ago in the fifth century BC."

"I wouldn't mind being a queen."

"And the bad guy in the story is named Haman. Haman," he repeated. "That almost sounds like Nathan."

"What's the story line?" Lisa asked.

"In short, Haman is the number two guy in the kingdom. And the one person he hates is this guy Mordecai—because Mordecai isn't afraid of him," said John Mark.

"That parallels with you and Nathan, doesn't it?" Lisa said. "I always had a hunch that Nathan felt intimidated by you. I mean, it only makes sense. You have expertise in both operations and sales. Nathan has expertise in neither."

"What's really ironic is that Nathan tried to get me transferred into the very job he ended up in," said John Mark.

"You never told me that," said Lisa.

"It didn't matter at the time," said John Mark. "He didn't get away with it anyway."

"But it *is* ironic," Lisa said.

"Yes, and it parallels with history because Haman ended up exactly in the place that he had planned for Mordecai to go."

"And what about the queen? You said she did the right thing. What was that?"

"She told the king that Haman had devised an evil plan."

Lisa's jaw dropped. "Really? That's in the story?"

"It's quite a parallel, isn't it?" said John Mark. "Esther was a Diplomat like you, and Mordecai a Strategist like me, and the king a Humanitarian like Max. You really ought to read the story. It's in the Old Testament. The book of Esther."

John Mark added, "But remember, it's only a rough parallel. If you study the actual history, you'll see that the differences are stark: You're not a queen like Esther, and Nathan is certainly not a tyrant like Haman."

"But was Haman a Diplomat like Nathan?" Lisa asked.

"As a matter of fact, he was."

"I've been wanting to ask you something," Lisa said. "How do you turn a narcissist around?"

"You don't," said John Mark. "I've become convinced that the antidote to narcissism is pain. Public pain. Huge embarrassment and disgrace. The all-important image has to crash."

"But sometimes even that is ineffective," Lisa said. "Remember the warden of the prison in the movie *The Shawshank Redemption*? He was narcissistic. But instead of paying the consequences of his choices, instead of undergoing the pain of being caught in the end, he pulled out a pistol and shot himself in the head."

"I don't think the People Model would've helped the warden," said John Mark. "The People Model only helps those who genuinely desire to develop into first-rate leaders. It only helps those who are willing to be changed inside their hearts. It's for people who want to be transformed."

"Do you think there's any hope for Nathan to get out of the basement?"

"We'll see how he responds to being fired," said John Mark. "This is his big opportunity. He has another chance to wake up."

"But will he?" Lisa asked.

"Did the warden?" replied John Mark.

"Not at all," Lisa answered. "Personally I can see why the warden killed himself. He would've gone to prison for life. His life at that juncture was hopeless."

"But there's another way of looking at it," said John Mark. "Think about the rest of the movie. It was a story of redemption and hope. Tim Robbins played a prisoner who was locked up for nineteen years, even though he was innocent of his alleged crime. Yet he rebuilt his life in the prison. And his best friend in the movie, the character played by Morgan Freeman, built a new life there too, though he was truly guilty of his crime."

"Okay, I see," said Lisa. "You're saying that the movie itself illustrates that it's possible to start fresh, even if you're in prison."

"That's right. And the warden could've done that too. But he chose selfishness instead."

Lisa responded, "I hope Nathan will become a new person."

"If he walks through the pain of his humiliation, then he will," said John Mark. "But if he blocks out the pain and pretends that all is well, then he won't."

"It might be best for Nathan, then, to take a time-out and sit on the bench for a while," said Lisa.

John Mark agreed.

"At the same time, it's too bad," said Lisa, "because he really is gifted."

"Yes, but Nathan has spent years winging it and faking it, and finally he's been caught," said John Mark. "It may take a long time for him to retool, especially if he decides to do some soul-searching."

"I think I'm ready to do some soul-searching," Lisa said.

"Are you saying that you're ready for a spiritual quest?"

"I don't know," said Lisa, "but I would like to be mentored more from your People Model."

"Well, then, let's plan for that."

"That sounds great," said Lisa.

Two weeks later, a companywide e-mail was sent out from the office of the president, announcing John Mark's new role. The message included strong words of commendation to everyone on the team for landing the biggest account in the history of the company.

In Max's next speech, he talked about the need to build a culture of support and accountability. "Together we can earn a worldwide reputation for the quality of our services," he said. "But we have to stick together because teamwork is the key to our success."

When Lisa heard him say this, she felt proud to be a member

of the company. Ever since Max had learned the truth about Nathan, *teamwork* had become his personal mantra.

As for Nathan, yes, he had been exposed and expelled. But by the time of Max's speech, Nathan had been named the new president of a medium-sized company that was searching for a figurehead to make it look impressive to the public.

PART THREE

THE
APPLICATION

CHAPTER 13

EXPLANATORY POWER

As I mentioned in the opening chapter, the People Model offers three different types of decision-making power: *explanatory power* to interpret organizational behavior, *motivational power* to muster up people's willingness to forfeit stubborn habits that have weakened their effectiveness in the past, and *creative power* to imagine wise solutions for the future. In these final three chapters, I will try to explain more clearly how the model can be used in all three practical ways.

First, the People Model helps people grow in self-awareness. This is what I mean by explanatory power. For example, most Strategists know they have a tendency to be critical and to slander. Likewise, most have probably been told that they can be judgmental at times. But what many may not see is their presumption. As John Mark figured out in the story, presumption is a form of impatience. Presumption is prejudgment, a type of self-righteous judgment that happens when a person fails to listen long enough to really understand what's going on.

Similarly, most Humanitarians realize that they tend to be people pleasers who often feel overly responsible. Most have also been told they can be indecisive at times. But what many may not see is their enablement of others. As Max came to realize in the story, enabling others' destructive behavior can destroy company culture. At root, enablement is self-serving. Enablement allows a downstairs Humanitarian to avoid the negative feelings he or she doesn't want to feel.

In the same way, most Diplomats know they have a tendency to promote and guard their images. Most have been told they can be dishonest at times. But what many may not see is their self-absorbed way of manipulating and intimidating people. As Lisa finally realized in the story, Nathan was attempting to get Max to push her out of senior leadership. Due to her self-absorption, she was slow to understand that Nathan's spin to Max was targeted strategically toward casting a dark shadow over her. The principle is timeless: Self-absorption causes people to prioritize themselves above others. Thus downstairs Diplomats are prone to take advantage of other people and use them for the sake of their own agendas.

On a similar note, the People Model helps people grow in their understanding of others. In other words, it helps people see the logical connection between values and behaviors. Whatever people value will determine their behavior. For instance, the Strategists' love for seeking truth causes them to be analytical. Because they're analytical, they tend to be confrontational as well. Whereas Strategists think it's productive to confront embarrassing issues, others in the company may prefer to avoid or ignore them.

In the same way, the Humanitarians' love for developing people causes them to be compassionate and forbearing. Because they're forbearing, they tend to be patient as well. Whereas Humanitarians are inclined to keep giving people second chances, others in the company may not be as hopeful or humane.

In like manner, the Diplomats' love for building unity causes them to be peaceable and calm. Because they're peaceable, they tend to be nonconfrontational as well. Whereas Diplomats want people to collaborate, others in the company may think it's unrealistic for alienated groups or traditional competitors to unite.

The Solutions Chart offers additional illustrations of the explanatory power of the People Model.

For instance, early in the narrative, John Mark uses the Strategists' solution to confront Nathan Gorman. Even when Nathan tries to deflect their conversations, John Mark focuses on the facts.

Cynthia, by contrast, generally uses the Humanitarians' solution. In the first lines of the story, Cynthia exercises empathy

SOLUTIONS CHART

STRATEGIST Solutions	HUMANITARIAN Solutions	DIPLOMAT Solutions
Be Bold.	Be Gracious.	Be Calm.
Identify the Problem.	Empathize with Those Involved.	Put the Problem in Perspective.
Expose the Problem.	Help the Person/Team in Need.	Wait. / Be Sensitive to the Timing.
Fix the Problem.	Forbear the Problem.	Finesse the Problem.
Speak up. / Confront.	Listen. / Be Patient.	Preface & Nuance Your Remarks.
Be Ethical.	Be Supportive.	Be Creative.
Be Real. / Offer Evidence.	Be Kind. / Do a Favor.	Be Generous. / Give a Gift.
Focus on the Facts.	Focus on People's Feelings.	Focus on the Setting & Mood.

when conversing with John Mark. Nevertheless, John Mark fails to empathize with her. Even so, she usually forbears him. When she doesn't, the two of them typically fight.

Empathy is rare in the business world. Yet empathetic listening can mitigate a number of costly problems. People who contend that they "just can't work together" often have a lack of empathy. Because they are unable to understand one another's feelings, they tend to be suspicious of each other. Though many leaders claim that emotions are irrelevant to the workplace, this very problem—the problem of invalidating other people's feelings—often stifles cooperation between coworkers.

In the narrative John Mark uses the Diplomats' solution as well. He uses it primarily with Lisa. He puts the problem of Nathan Gorman in perspective, nuances his remarks, and waits until the right moment to prod Lisa to be bold and speak up.

Furthermore, the People Model explains why perennial tensions exist between people in different columns of the basement. A prominent example is the tension that persists between below-the-line Strategists and below-the-line Diplomats. While below-the-line Strategists tend to be prideful and self-righteous, below-the-line Diplomats tend to be vainglorious and deceitful. The dishonesty of the Diplomats triggers the self-righteousness of the Strategists.

Consider the dynamics in the story. The drama begins with Max enabling Nathan's dishonest behavior. After that the basement problems snowball. Nathan hides the truth by pretending to be loyal to Max. When John Mark catches on to Nathan's feigned devotion, John Mark becomes angry at him. The angrier he becomes, the more he slanders Nathan Gorman and justifies himself. To his credit, however, John Mark confronts Nathan in private, exercising reason and self-control. But Nathan feels threatened by this. As a result, Nathan redeploys John Mark, and Max allows Nathan to get away with it.

This complex scenario reveals a major principle—below-the-line leadership typically infects the whole team. When Nathan fell into the basement, so did Max, and then John Mark, and then Lisa. Yet this domino effect can go either way. As the narrative illustrates, above-the-line leadership promotes above-the-line performance of the team. When John Mark rose above the line, others in the story did too. This principle explains why good character is the key to good leadership.

CHAPTER 14

MOTIVATIONAL
POWER

The People Model offers motivational power to help people desire to rise above the line. When I present the model in person, I like to ask the audience, as an opening exercise, to select their favorite expression (shown below). So let me pose the same question to you: If you could only choose one, which statement promises the wisdom you desire most for yourself?

Discovering Your Blind Spots: A Guide to Finding the Truth That You Don't See

Salvaging Your Blunders: A Guide to Recovering Your Mistakes

Covering Your Blemishes: A Guide to Being More Winsome and Attractive

Okay, hold on to your answer, and I'll explain exactly how the People Model works. It enables you to see that what you *least* want to do is the very thing that will make you a better leader.

Allow me to elaborate. Many times people take refuge in the basement. They stay there because they honestly believe that their critics are mistaking their above-the-line qualities for below-the-line qualities.

So many times, for instance, Strategists are told to chill out and become more agreeable. They are urged, so to speak, to turn the light off, sit with everyone else in the dark, and pretend that all is fine. But Strategists have no interest in pretending that all is well when all is not. Consequently, Strategists become defensive whenever they are told to tolerate something that seems utterly intolerable to them. So how do you get a prideful Strategist to be humble? How do you help Strategists see the damage that their arrogance incurs? The matter is complex because those who label Strategists as "stubborn" and "judgmental" are usually the same critics who discount their contribution of upholding high standards and tackling crippling problems head-on.

The same principle applies to Humanitarians. So many times Humanitarians are told to toughen up and move more quickly. They are urged, so to speak, to raise the temperature in the company, focus less on people, and run a tighter ship. But Humanitarians have no interest in setting aside their fear of displeasing people—because they are too afraid to take that risk. Consequently, Humanitarians become defensive whenever they are told to toughen up and move more quickly and decisively. So how can you get a fearful Humanitarian to be bold? How do you help Humanitarians to understand how costly their guilt and fear can really be? The matter is complex because those who berate Humanitarians for being "weak" and "indecisive" are usually the same critics who discount their contribution of prioritizing people and making the company culture humane.

The same goes for the Diplomats. So many times the Diplomats are told to communicate more openly and truthfully. They are urged, so to speak, to stop decorating their words and start being blunter and less tactful. But Diplomats have no interest in devaluing the importance of being sensitive to the timing and the manner in which things are said. Consequently, Diplomats become defensive whenever they are urged to proclaim the naked truth. So how can you get a Diplomat to be honest? How do you help Diplomats to truly understand how destructive their spin can be? The matter is complex because those who accuse them of being "full of themselves" and "manipulative" are usually the same critics who discount their contribution of uniting people groups and formulating a peaceable perspective.

Because of all these things, countless individuals do not change. They stay stuck below the line because they lack the motivation to rise above it. To many, the price of changing seems too costly. It appears to them that rising above the line means forfeiting their values, letting go of their most cherished ideals.

Here's what I mean by that. For Strategists, it may seem that the only way to stop being stubborn and judgmental is to stop embracing truth and authenticity. For Humanitarians, it may seem that the only way to stop being weak and indecisive is to stop embracing goodness and compassion. For Diplomats it may seem that the only way to stop being full of themselves and manipulative is to stop embracing harmony and peace.

So how do you motivate people to risk letting go of their character flaws? I believe the answer is this: You figure out a way to appeal to their below-the-line values and their above-the-line values simultaneously. For example, you aim at the Strategists' pride, but also at their desire to know the truth. Likewise, you aim at the Humanitarians' fear, but also at their desire to be compassionate. In the same way, you aim at the Diplomats' vanity, but also at their desire to bring peace. In other words, you come up with a marketing phrase that promises to deliver two vital things: what people *want* and what people *need.*

Let's start with the Strategists. What they want is better vision. They want insight and answers. They want to see life with new eyes. So here's the tailor-made title for the Strategists—*Discovering Your Blind Spots: A Guide to Finding the Truth That You Don't See.* Whether Strategists are above the line (championing truth) or below the line (mistakenly presuming they already have it), the promise of discovering their blind spots is compelling.

But what do the Strategists need? They need humility. What better way is there to motivate Strategists to humble themselves than by promising to give them better vision? When Strategists humble themselves, they generate new insights. They distinguish their opinions from their values. They grow in self-awareness. They realize things they've never seen before. Humility gives people new eyes. It enables them to see that when they are self-righteously judgmental, their best judgment is impaired.

Next, let's examine the Humanitarians. What the Humanitarians want is to make the world a better place. They want to value people and help them feel as comfortable as possible. And yet Humanitarians can feel so overly responsible that they quickly fall into guilt if someone is ever hurt instead of helped. So here's the specially-made title for the Humanitarians—*Salvaging Your Blunders: A Guide to Recovering Your Mistakes.* Whether Humanitarians are above the line (empowering people) or below the line (enabling people), the promise of salvaging their blunders is compelling.

But what do the Humanitarians need? They need courage.

What better incentive is there to make Humanitarians want to be courageous than by promising to make them more helpful? When Humanitarians understand that loyalty and kindness are *not* dismissed by truthfulness and confrontation, they can muster up the courage to be bold. They can challenge unwieldy voices and say the hard thing. They can fight against the pressure to be complicit. Courage gives people new resolve. It emboldens them to search for core solutions rather than putting Band-Aids on big problems. Courage strengthens Humanitarians so they can take a stand for what is right.

Finally, let's consider the Diplomats. What the Diplomats want is to transcend the ugliness that comes when peace and unity are violated. They want order and proportion. They want people to be civil and united. They want to be persuasive, not offensive. So here's the custom-made title for the Diplomats: *Covering Your Blemishes: A Guide to Being More Winsome and Attractive.* Whether Diplomats are above the line (uniting people) or below the line (using people), the promise of covering their blemishes is compelling.

And what do the Diplomats need? They need honesty. What better way is there to motivate Diplomats to be honest than by promising to make them more winsome? When Diplomats see that honesty is refreshing and that people are attracted to leaders who are real instead of plastic, then they can dare to speak the truth. They can throw away their masks and find new self-acceptance. They can participate with others without pretending to be something they are not. Honesty gives people credibility. It increases self-respect and makes people more respectable to others.

How did I figure out everything I just now explained? The People Model told me. According to the People Model, there are three besetting issues that cause a person or organization to be ineffective: pride, fear, and deceitfulness. Logically, we can guess what the solution has to be for each vice. If the problem is pride, then the solution is *humility*. If the problem is fear, the solution must be *courage*. If the problem is deceitfulness, the solution must be *honesty*.

	STRATEGISTS (Light)	HUMANITARIANS (Temp)	DIPLOMATS (Color)
	Self-Righteous	Self-Serving	Self-Absorbed
	Criticism, Harshness	People Pleasing	Image Management
	IS THREATENING	IS WEAK	IS MANIPULATIVE
BEHAVIOR:	Self-Righteous Judgment —Slander —Presumption —Impatience	Enablement —Gossip —Guilt Trips —Martyr Complex	Spin (Spin Club) —Distorts, Redefines Truth —Political Intimidation —Victim of Circumstances
THE PROBLEM:	PRIDE	FEAR	DECEITFULNESS
THE ANTIDOTE:	HUMILITY	COURAGE	HONESTY

The motivational power of the People Model, then, is that it offers an incentive to help people move from pride to humility, from fear to courage, and from deceitfulness to honesty.

CHAPTER 15

CREATIVE
POWER

The People Model also has creative power that offers practical solutions to common problems. Perhaps the best way to discover how its power can be applied is to exercise the model yourself. You can use the Solutions Chart as you ponder what you would do in each scenario described below.

    a. You're introducing a big change in the company, and one department in particular keeps complaining about it.

    b. Your supervisor (or the chair of the board) gives a lame excuse for having made a mistake that causes you to redo two weeks of work and makes you look bad to a few people inside the company.

    c. Your teenage son tells you that he wants to quit high

school, move to Hollywood, and try to "be discovered" as an actor.

d. Your spouse bounces a check from your joint bank account.

SOLUTIONS CHART

STRATEGIST Solutions	HUMANITARIAN Solutions	DIPLOMAT Solutions
Be Bold.	Be Gracious.	Be Calm.
Identify the Problem.	Empathize with Those Involved.	Put the Problem in Perspective.
Expose the Problem.	Help the Person/Team in Need.	Wait. / Be Sensitive to the Timing.
Fix the Problem.	Forbear the Problem.	Finesse the Problem.
Speak up. / Confront.	Listen. / Be Patient.	Preface & Nuance Your Remarks.
Be Ethical.	Be Supportive.	Be Creative.
Be Real. / Offer Evidence.	Be Kind. / Do a Favor.	Be Generous. / Give a Gift.
Focus on the Facts.	Focus on People's Feelings.	Focus on the Setting & Mood.

Since first-rate leaders need to be developed in all three categories, it's imperative to learn how to lead above the line in all three categories. Every situation allows a leader to be humble, courageous, and honest. But since most situations are complex, most situations call for creativity and imagination. Most of the time the only way to synthesize the strengths in all three categories is for the leader to be sensitive to the *ordering* of the solutions that are applied.

For example, if we look at line two in the Solutions Chart and read it horizontally, we can readily see that it's possible—even advisable—for a leader to apply all three solutions provided. In other words, a leader can identify the problem, empathize with the people involved, and also put the problem into perspective.

But since a leader cannot do that all at once, the leader has to order the solutions in sequence.

Let's say, for example, that the leader is primarily a Strategist.
In that case, it would probably be most natural for the leader to
identify the problem. If the leader, however, is primarily a Humanitarian, then it probably would be difficult to identify the problem
because the leader would be focused more on empathy than analysis, at least at first. If the leader is primarily a Diplomat, the leader
would see the problem differently. Whereas the Strategist would
identity the problem as a problem, the Diplomat might try to minimize it or hide it. The Strategist, by contrast, might exaggerate the
problem and see things out of proportion. It's interesting to note
that both the Strategist and Diplomat are liable to forget about
helping the people involved. The Humanitarian, on the other
hand, may struggle to put the problem in perspective because of
his or her tendency to try to please too many people at once.

Given these tendencies, it's important for leaders to be conscious of their primary category because that heightens their
awareness of the solutions they're less likely to employ. For a
leader to imagine creative solutions, the leader needs to learn how
to maneuver from point to point and line to line on the Solutions
Chart.

To illustrate, allow me to be more specific. Suppose a supervisor is leading the organization through a big transition, and
one department in particular is complaining rather than cooperating. Though there are many ways to sequence the solutions on
the Solutions Chart, an above-the-line Humanitarian might do
well to start with the Diplomats' solution. Thus she would begin
by detaching herself from the situation at hand, and thereby stay
calm, cool, and collected rather than overly connected to the
emotions of her coworkers. If that Humanitarian continued to

use the Solutions Chart as a guide, she might choose to act in the following sequence:

1. *Be calm.*
2. *Identify the problem (or challenge).*
3. *Put the problem (or challenge) in perspective.*
4. *Wait. Be sensitive to the timing of when to address the disgruntled group.*
5. *Be gracious.*
6. *Empathize with those involved.*
7. *Be supportive.*
8. *Speak up.*

Then what? Will she attempt to fix the problem, forbear the problem, or finesse the problem? It's impossible to do all three simultaneously. Thus she is faced with a decision. Let's say, for the sake of example, that she chooses to:

9. *Preface and nuance her remarks.*
10. *Be bold.*
11. *Expose the problem.*
12. *Fix the problem—which in this case means she effects the big change rather than cowing down to the complainers.*

The point is worth repeating—both the People Model and the Solutions Chart call for imagination from the leader. The leader has to use his or her imagination to envision how the sequencing of the solutions might play out.

Consider a second example. Let's say a Strategist learns that his teenage son wants to quit high school, move to Hollywood, and attempt to make it big as an actor. After consulting the Solutions Chart, let's say the father decides to:

1. *Be gracious.*
2. *Listen (without asking any probing questions). Be patient.*
3. *Empathize with his son's feelings.*
4. *Identify the problem privately to himself.*
5. *Wait. Be sensitive to the timing.*
6. *Focus on the setting and mood.*
7. *Speak up.*
8. *Expose the problem.*
9. *Preface and nuance his remarks to his son.*
10. *Help his son.*
11. *Be creative.*
12. *Finesse the problem.*

Third example. Let's say a Diplomat's supervisor gives a lame excuse for having made a mistake that forces her to redo two weeks of work and makes her look bad inside the company. How might she respond if she follows the Solutions Chart?

1. *Wait.*
2. *Put the problem in perspective.*
3. *Be sensitive to the timing.*
4. *Focus on the mood or setting.*
5. *Speak up.*
6. *Preface her remarks.*
7. *Speak up again by asking questions to find out what really happened.*
8. *Listen. Be patient.*

9. Empathize with the person who made the mistake.

10. Identify the problem behind the problem.

11. Be gracious.

12. Forbear the problem.

See the flexibility of the Solutions Chart? The Solutions Chart offers countless ways of sequencing solutions. The solutions in each column are available to everyone, regardless of the leader's primary type. The same thing can be said of the elements above the line in the People Model chart.

The flexibility of the People Model is one of its greatest strengths. Still, as John Mark reminded Cynthia in the story, the People Model is only a tool. It has no power unless you choose to pick it up, learn how it can work for you, and creatively apply it to the unique situations you face.

FINAL INSIGHTS

Having lived with the People Model for eighteen months, I can say from experience that it continually provides new insights. Most recently I realized that conflicts between people of different categories are not mere clashes of values. Rather, they are conflicts over values in which people take security.

For instance, the Strategists want the organization to be authentic because they take security in other people's authenticity. When someone fails to be authentic (i.e., true to the company's mission), the Strategist may react—not because the Strategist can't handle other people making mistakes per se, but rather because the Strategist's personal security is threatened. For a Strategist, it makes no sense even to have a company unless its members are committed to its primary purpose for existing. It's all about the mission for the Strategist. So when someone breaches the mission, the Strategist may question whether that person rightly belongs on the team. Of course, a Humanitarian or Diplomat may also be concerned if someone disregards the mission routinely. But for the Strategist the problem is more visceral. It bothers the Strategist—at an emotional level—because the Strategist takes security in having everyone be true to the company's purpose.

Humanitarians, by contrast, want the organization to be a comfortable community because they take security in other people's comfortable feelings. Said in reverse, Humanitarians feel uncomfortable when others are outside their comfort zones. That is not to suggest that Humanitarians can't handle it when members of the company complain or withdraw. The point is, rather, that Humanitarians' sense of security is bound up with the feelings of others. So when a team member feels hurt, a Humanitarian may react by becoming too protective of that person, even at the expense of the organization's mission. Of course, a Strategist or Diplomat may be overly protective of particular individuals as well. But, relatively speaking, the Humanitarians' protectiveness of hurt people in the company runs deeper. The reason why, as we now know, is because Humanitarians take security in having others feel accepted and at ease.

As for the Diplomats, they want the organization to be impressive because they take security in the projection of positive images. That is not to say that Diplomats can't handle unpolished coworkers. It's rather to point out that negative projections shake the Diplomat's sense of security. For a Diplomat, it's useless for an entity to be well-known if its public reputation works against it. It's useless to work hard if no one is impressed—or if no one knows the company exists. So when someone is perceived as being a threat to the organization's image, a Diplomat might react by undervaluing that person's contribution, even if he or she has a solid track record of forwarding the company's mission. Of course, a Strategist or Humanitarian would also be concerned if someone regularly embarrassed the organization. But for Diplomats, the problem is more upsetting since it rattles them internally and causes them to feel too vulnerable.

So what does all this mean? It means that value clashes are emotionally loaded because people's sense of security is at stake.

I am confident, therefore, that emotionally charged value clashes can be well managed when people take pains to respect and understand the basis of their security, and especially when they choose to place their ultimate security in God.

If you think about it, all three values I've described are legitimate. All three deserve to be respected and pursued. All three are reflective of God. God cares about authenticity because God himself is truth. He cares about people's feelings because He is compassionate and good. He cares about harmony and order (the very elements that make things impressive) because he is a God of beauty. Heaven and earth alike attest to that.

I've noticed something else. The People Model serves as a marvelous grid for generating insights from the Bible. Take just one example, 1 Corinthians 13, the famous love chapter in the New Testament. In effect, it says:

> *If I speak with the artful tongue of a Diplomat and can dazzle those around me by building unity between groups and exhibiting great charisma and finesse . . . but do not have love, I have become a noisy gong or a clanging cymbal.*
>
> *And if I am a masterful Strategist who can analyze complex issues, think clearly in a storm and act boldly*

and decisively with integrity . . . but do not have love,
I am nothing.

And if I am heroic, a tireless Humanitarian who sac-
rifices everything for the sake of other people, even to the
point of laying down my life as a martyr . . . but do not
have love, it profits me nothing.

The wisdom of this passage is reflected in the People Model chart. Tacitly the chart says you can think you're above the line—but unless your motives are unselfish, you're actually in the basement being self-righteous or self-serving or self-absorbed.

In other words, if you think you're above the line in the Strategist category, but you don't have love, you're actually being presumptuous and self-righteous. Likewise, you can think you're above the line in the Humanitarian category if you're patient and kind and loyal. But if you're motivated by people pleasing rather than genuine love, then really you are being self-serving. In the same way, you can think you're above the line in the Diplomat category if you're uniting everybody and finagling your way out of problems. But if you're doing so without love, then in truth you're self-absorbed.

Love, by definition, is unselfish. It takes love to produce a humble Strategist, a courageous Humanitarian, and an honest Diplomat. Love is the key to leadership above the line.

If you want more information,
feel free to check out the Web site
www.leadershipabovetheline.com.

ACKNOWLEDGMENTS

Many people helped me with this book. To begin with, there was Kimberley Wiedefeld, my mentoree, who encouraged me to take the model seriously. If it weren't for her, I may have simply kept it to myself. On the night I first explained it, she urged me to record it on paper. I needed her prodding. It had not occurred to me that anyone else might value my reflections. Granted, I knew it constituted a major breakthrough when I realized the distinction between Truth language and Beauty language (I had been pondering John Keats's words, "Beauty is truth, truth beauty."). But I honestly didn't see that a full model—the People Model—was nestled in my brain until Kimberley tugged at me. She and I enjoyed an unforgettable evening that went late into the night mining out the model from my head.

Next, I want to thank Jan Long Harris at Tyndale House

Publishers who played a major role behind the scenes. Jan has a special knack for assessing ideas and knowing which ones to keep. She raised the bar on five crucial aspects of this book. I am indebted to her. I am also very grateful because months before I even started writing the book, Jan believed in me enough to rally a circle of colleagues to hear a two-hour presentation of the People Model. All five Tyndale members cheered me on: Jan, Doug, Joan, Caleb, and Nancy.

Then came the work of two of my former students, Tracy Benelli and Daniel Eichelberger. Tracy endured the worst rendition of the manuscript. Her editing lifted the project to an entirely different level. Daniel twice refined it and proofread the final version just before the book went to print.

Along with that came a number of gracious readers whose input influenced me: Felix Gambini, Robert Harvey, Haley Henningson, Kristina Khederlarian, Deanna Leach, Joel Lehman, Susan Lied, Lou Markos, Sandy Miller, Ted Powl, Matthew Sayovitz, La Verne Tolbert, Gail Wallace, Jon Wallace, and Kimberley Wiedefeld. Special thanks to Richard and Susan Andersen, Luellen Lucid, Ben White, and Jim Stockham, all of whom read more than one iteration and spent time discussing the manuscript with me. Mike Hughes and Greg Nettle, likewise, were each generous enough to comment on it line by line. I literally implemented every single change that Mike suggested early on and that Greg suggested later.

I also want to thank three staff members who work outside my office. It's funny to me now: Ismari, Barb, and Marilyn disliked every working title I suggested until, as a last resort, I tossed out one more possible idea, *Leadership above the Line*. Suddenly they gave a thumbs-up. I was staggered by their positive response. Finally, I had captured a good title. That moment went down in history for me.

Then came the input of Barb Hayes, Nancy Jordan, Michelle Sayovitz, Michael Whyte, David Wright, and Dave Ridley. Together their remarks catalyzed my thoughts and helped me to produce the final manuscript. There were many rounds of revisions, but with every subsequent rewrite, the manuscript improved significantly.

I am particularly honored that Gayle Beebe wrote the foreword. I asked him to write it because he is a first-rate leader. The wisdom he offered as I prepared the manuscript not only helped the book, but helped me personally as a leader. I am truly humbled by the privilege of having his influence in my life.

Indispensable to the process was Kim Miller, my editor. Her expertise, her patience, her tremendous eye for detail as well as her steady work ethic made the whole process heartening and enjoyable for me. Consistently her feedback was helpful. Kim is an excellent editor. I gained so much from our lengthy and unhurried conversations. She challenged me with high standards yet supported me with her guidance and understanding. I welcome the opportunity to work with her again in the future.

I struggle to find the words to thank my husband, Jim Sumner. He has helped me more than anyone to rise above the line in my own life. He's my cheerleader and my coach. He prompts me to go forward, step-by-step, in my development as a follower of Christ. I truly couldn't ask for a better partner.

Ultimately, my gratitude goes to God. He alone inspired me, not only with the idea of the People Model itself, but also with the energy to write. For me, the arduous process of bringing forth this book proved to be profoundly transformative.

PART FOUR

THE
TOOLS

THE PEOPLE
MODEL TEST

There are three versions of the People Model test. Actually, they are identical, except for the lead-in questions, which are tailored to the person taking the test. The test is a simple, nonscientific tool that can be used informally to help you determine what People Model category best describes you as an individual or your organization (or family) as a whole. (See page 178). The test can also be used to assess your behavior in a particular circumstance or situation. (Note: Since everyone is a mix of all three categories, it's possible, for instance, for someone who is primarily a Humanitarian to act as a Strategist in a given situation.)

To maximize the benefit of the test, ask one or two other people to take it on your behalf, so you can see if your perceptions of yourself match theirs. (See page 176 for an evaluation they can use.) Be sure to let them know if you're testing yourself overall or testing yourself in a given situation with which the evaluator is familiar. Please note: Evaluations are likely to be most accurate if evaluators have read *Leadership above the Line*.

THE PEOPLE MODEL TEST: PERSONAL

This test is a tool to evaluate you as an individual. It can also be used to evaluate your behavior in a particular situation. (Note: Since everyone is a mix of all three categories, it's possible, for instance, for someone who is primarily a Humanitarian to act as a Strategist. It all depends upon the situation.)

DIRECTIONS
Evaluate the word sets below by marking the one that *more often than not* describes you best with a 3, second-best with a 2, and the least with a 1. Fill in all the blanks, even if all or none of the word sets seem to describe you accurately.

What's more important to you?

1. _____ a. Personal integrity   _____ b. Compassion for other people   _____ c. A good reputation

2. _____ a. Belonging and togetherness   _____ b. Harmony and peace   _____ c. Quality and high standards

3. _____ a. Being refined in your manner of speech   _____ b. Being supplied with relevant data   _____ c. Being sensitive to others

4. _____ a. Developing people   _____ b. Identifying the root of a problem   _____ c. Unifying people

5. _____ a. That your team be principled   _____ b. That your team be impressive   _____ c. That your team feels comfortable

When you are struggling with a problem, you are more likely to:

6. _____ a. Be nervous   _____ b. Be aloof   _____ c. Be cynical

7. _____ a. Redefine the truth   _____ b. Judge someone else   _____ c. Excuse others' bad behavior

8. _____ a. Blame others   _____ b. Blame yourself   _____ c. Blame no one

9. _____ a. Clean up the mess   _____ b. Hide the mess   _____ c. Prevent the mess from happening again

10. _____ a. Focus on the timing of your response   _____ b. Confront the problem head-on   _____ c. Help the person(s) struggling with the problem

At your best, you are more likely to be:

11. _____ a. Gentle   _____ b. Spirited   _____ c. Calm

12. _____ a. Analytical   _____ b. Relational   _____ c. Winsome

13. _____ a. Authentic   _____ b. Refined   _____ c. Loyal

14. _____ a. Kind and understanding   _____ b. Uncompromising and clear   _____ c. Tactful and adroit at handling conflict

15. _____ a. Able to network   _____ b. Able to solve a problem   _____ c. Able to give generously of yourself for the sake of others

DATE COMPLETED: ___ / ___ / _____   THIS TEST IS AN EVALUATION OF: _____

THIS EVALUATION IS: ☐ general   ☐ limited to a specific situation

If it is limited to a specific situation, then describe very briefly what that situation is, so that in the future you don't forget the meaning of these test results.

_____

_____

When you are at your worst, you are more likely to:

16. _✗_ a. Intimidate   ____ b. Gossip   ____ c. Slander

17. ____ a. Be presumptuous   ____ b. Be indecisive   _✗_ c. Be manipulative

18. ____ a. Be self-absorbed   _✗_ b. Be self-righteous ____ c. Be self-preserving

19. ____ a. Be afraid   ____ b. Be deceitful   _✗_ c. Be prideful

20. _✗_ a. Interrupt others   ____ b. Flatter others   ____ c. Coddle others

TEST RESULTS

Transfer your numeric answers from the test to the results sheet on this page. Then tally the totals. The higher your score in column 1, the more of a Strategist you are. The higher your score in column 2, the more of a Humanitarian you are. The higher your score in column 3, the more of a Diplomat you are.

Reminder: How you act in any given situation may vary. At work you may operate primarily in a different category than you do when you're at home. Overall, however, people have a natural tendency to be predominant in one category.

Strategists	Humanitarians	Diplomats
1. a = ____	1. b = _✗_	1. c = ____
2. c = _✗_	2. a = ____	2. b = ____
3. b = ____	3. c = _✗_	3. a = ____
4. b = ____	4. a = _✗_	4. c = ____
5. a = ____	5. c = _✗_	5. b = ____
6. c = _✗_	6. a = ____	6. b = ____
7. b = _✗_	7. c = ____	7. a = ____
8. a = _✗_	8. b = ____	8. c = ____
9. c = _✗_	9. a = ____	9. b = ____
10. b = _✗_	10. c = ____	10. a = _✗_
11. b = _✗_	11. a = ____	11. c = _✗_
12. a = ____	12. b = ____	12. c = _✗_
13. a = _✗_	13. c = ____	13. b = ____
14. b = ____	14. a = _✗_	14. c = ____
15. b = ____	15. c = _✗_	15. a = ____
16. c = ____	16. b = ____	16. a = _✗_
17. a = ____	17. b = ____	17. c = _✗_
18. b = _✗_	18. c = ____	18. a = ____
19. c = _✗_	19. a = ____	19. b = ____
20. a = _✗_	20. c = ____	20. b = ____
Total = _11_	Total = _0_	Total = _6_

THE PEOPLE MODEL TEST: OBSERVER

This test is a tool to evaluate an individual. It can also be used to evaluate someone's behavior in a particular situation. (Note: Since everyone is a mix of all three categories, it's possible, for instance, for someone who is primarily a Humanitarian to act as a Strategist. It all depends upon the situation.)

DIRECTIONS

Evaluate the word sets below by marking a 3 next to the word that *more often than not* best describes the person you're evaluating. Mark 2 for the second-best answer. Mark 1 for the word that describes him or her the least. Fill in all the blanks, even if you don't think any of the words seem to fit closely. Remember to evaluate the person either on his or her behavior overall or according to a specific situation, if that is detailed.

What's more important to this individual?

1. _____ a. Personal integrity   _____ b. Compassion for other   _____ c. A good reputation
   people

2. _____ a. Belonging and   _____ b. Harmony and peace   _____ c. Quality and high standards
   togetherness

3. _____ a. Being refined in his or   _____ b. Being supplied with   _____ c. Being sensitve to others
   her manner of speech   relevant data

4. _____ a. Developing people   _____ b. Identifying the root   _____ c. Unifying people
   of a problem

5. _____ a. That his or her team   _____ b. That his or her team   _____ c. That his or her team
   be principled   be impressive   feels comfortable

When this person is struggling with a problem, he or she is more likely to:

6. _____ a. Be nervous   _____ b. Be aloof   _____ c. Be cynical

7. _____ a. Redefine the truth   _____ b. Judge someone else   _____ c. Excuse others' bad
   behavior

8. _____ a. Blame others   _____ b. Blame himself   _____ c. Blame no one
   or herself

9. _____ a. Clean up the mess   _____ b. Hide the mess   _____ c. Prevent the mess from
   happening again

10. _____ a. Focus on the timing   _____ b. Confront the problem   _____ c. Help the person(s)
    of his or her response   head-on   struggling with the problem

At this person's best, he or she is more likely to be:

11. _____ a. Gentle   _____ b. Spirited   _____ c. Calm

12. _____ a. Analytical   _____ b. Relational   _____ c. Winsome

13. _____ a. Authentic   _____ b. Refined   _____ c. Loyal

14. _____ a. Kind and   _____ b. Uncompromising   _____ c. Tactful and adroit at
    understanding   and clear   handling conflict

15. _____ a. Able to network   _____ b. Able to solve a problem   _____ c. Able to give generously
    for the sake of others

When this person is at his or her worst, he or she is most likely to:

16. ____ a. Intimidate	____ b. Gossip	____ c. Slander
17. ____ a. Be presumptuous	____ b. Be indecisive	____ c. Be manipulative
18. ____ a. Be self-absorbed	____ b. Be self-righteous	____ c. Be self-preserving
19. ____ a. Be afraid	____ b. Be deceitful	____ c. Be prideful
20. ____ a. Interrupt others	____ b. Flatter others	____ c. Coddle others

TEST RESULTS

Transfer the numeric answers from the test to the results sheet on this page. Then tally the totals. The higher a person scores in column 1, the more of a Strategist he or she is. The higher a person scores in column 2, the more of a Humanitarian he or she is. The higher a person scores in column 3, the more of a Diplomat he or she is.

Reminder: How one acts in any given situation may vary. At work a person may operate primarily in a different category than when he or she is at home. Overall, however, people have a natural tendency to be predominant in one category.

Strategists	Humanitarians	Diplomats
1. a = ____	1. b = ____	1. c = ____
2. c = ____	2. a = ____	2. b = ____
3. b = ____	3. c = ____	3. a = ____
4. b = ____	4. a = ____	4. c = ____
5. a = ____	5. c = ____	5. b = ____
6. c = ____	6. a = ____	6. b = ____
7. b = ____	7. c = ____	7. a = ____
8. a = ____	8. b = ____	8. c = ____
9. c = ____	9. a = ____	9. b = ____
10. b = ____	10. c = ____	10. a = ____
11. b = ____	11. a = ____	11. c = ____
12. a = ____	12. b = ____	12. c = ____
13. a = ____	13. c = ____	13. b = ____
14. b = ____	14. a = ____	14. c = ____
15. b = ____	15. c = ____	15. a = ____
16. c = ____	16. b = ____	16. a = ____
17. a = ____	17. b = ____	17. c = ____
18. b = ____	18. c = ____	18. a = ____
19. c = ____	19. a = ____	19. b = ____
20. a = ____	20. c = ____	20. b = ____
Total = ____	Total = ____	Total = ____

THE PEOPLE MODEL TEST: ORGANIZATION

This test is a tool to evaluate an organization. It can also be used to evaluate an organization's behavior in a particular situation. (Note: Since an organization is a mix of all three categories, it's possible, for instance, for a company that primarily operates in the Humanitarian category to act as a Strategist in a certain instance. It all depends upon the situation.)

DIRECTIONS

Evaluate the word sets below by marking a 3 next to the word set that *more often than not* best describes the organization you're evaluating. Mark 2 for the second-best answer. Mark 1 for the word set that describes the organization least. Fill in all the blanks, even if you don't think any of the word sets seem to fit closely. Remember to evaluate the organization either on its behavior overall or according to a specific situation, if that is detailed.

What's more important to your organization?

1. _____ a. Personal integrity   _____ b. Compassion for people   _____ c. A good reputation
2. _____ a. Belonging and togetherness   _____ b. Harmony and peace   _____ c. Quality and high standards
3. _____ a. Being refined in its manner of speech   _____ b. Being supplied with relevant data   _____ c. Being sensitive to others
4. _____ a. Developing people   _____ b. Identifying the root of a problem   _____ c. Unifying people
5. _____ a. That teams be principled   _____ b. That teams be impressive   _____ c. That teams feel comfortable

When your organization faces a problem, it is more likely to:

6. _____ a. Be nervous   _____ b. Be aloof   _____ c. Be cynical
7. _____ a. Redefine the truth   _____ b. Judge someone else   _____ c. Excuse others' bad behavior
8. _____ a. Blame others   _____ b. Blame itself   _____ c. Blame no one
9. _____ a. Clean up the mess   _____ b. Hide the mess   _____ c. Prevent the mess from happening again
10. _____ a. Focus on the timing of its response   _____ b. Confront the problem head-on   _____ c. Help the person(s) struggling with the problem

At your organization's best, it is more likely to be:

11. _____ a. Gentle   _____ b. Spirited   _____ c. Calm
12. _____ a. Analytical   _____ b. Relational   _____ c. Winsome
13. _____ a. Authentic   _____ b. Refined   _____ c. Loyal
14. _____ a. Kind and understanding   _____ b. Uncompromising and clear   _____ c. Tactful and adroit at handling conflict
15. _____ a. Able to network   _____ b. Able to solve a problem   _____ c. Able to give generously for the sake of others

When your organization is at its worst, it is most likely to:

16. ____ a. Intimidate   ____ b. Gossip   ____ c. Slander

17. ____ a. Be presumptuous   ____ b. Be indecisive   ____ c. Be manipulative

18. ____ a. Be self-absorbed   ____ b. Be self-righteous   ____ c. Be self-preserving

19. ____ a. Be afraid   ____ b. Be deceitful   ____ c. Be prideful

20. ____ a. Interrupt others   ____ b. Flatter others   ____ c. Coddle others

TEST RESULTS

Transfer the numeric answers from the test to the results sheet on this page. Then tally the totals. The higher an organization scores in column 1, the more Strategic it is. The higher an organization scores in column 2, the more Humanitarian it is. The higher an organization scores in column 3, the more Diplomatic it is.

Reminder: How a company acts in any given situation may vary. Overall, however, organizational cultures have a natural tendency to be predominant in one category.

Strategists	Humanitarians	Diplomats
1. a = ____	1. b = ____	1. c = ____
2. c = ____	2. a = ____	2. b = ____
3. b = ____	3. c = ____	3. a = ____
4. b = ____	4. a = ____	4. c = ____
5. a = ____	5. c = ____	5. b = ____
6. c = ____	6. a = ____	6. b = ____
7. b = ____	7. c = ____	7. a = ____
8. a = ____	8. b = ____	8. c = ____
9. c = ____	9. a = ____	9. b = ____
10. b = ____	10. c = ____	10. a = ____
11. b = ____	11. a = ____	11. c = ____
12. a = ____	12. b = ____	12. c = ____
13. a = ____	13. c = ____	13. b = ____
14. b = ____	14. a = ____	14. c = ____
15. b = ____	15. c = ____	15. a = ____
16. c = ____	16. b = ____	16. a = ____
17. a = ____	17. b = ____	17. c = ____
18. b = ____	18. c = ____	18. a = ____
19. c = ____	19. a = ____	19. b = ____
20. a = ____	20. c = ____	20. b = ____
Total = ____	Total = ____	Total = ____

THE PEOPLE MODEL

	STRATEGISTS (Light)	HUMANITARIANS (Temp)	DIPLOMATS (Color)
	Explanatory Power	Motivational Power	Creative Power
VIEWPOINT:	2nd Person (You) —Operational	3rd Person (He, She, They) —Cultural	1st Person (I, We) —Political
	Freedom	Compassion	Peace
	Authentic Community	Comfortable Community	Impressive Community
	Be Good	Feel Good	Look Good
	Clarity, Accountability	Develop, Support People	Sense of Harmony and Order
	Integrity	Togetherness	Unity
	Straightforward Message	Wise Approach	Wise Timing
	Confrontational, Spirited	Forbearing, Gentle	Nonconfrontational, Calm
	Discerning, Analytical	Patient, Kind	Finesse, Artful Demeanor
PERCEPTION:	SEEMS THREATENING	SEEMS WEAK	SEEMS MANIPULATIVE
	Corrective	Loyal	Polished, Refined
PRIORITY:	INFRASTRUCTURE	SERVICE	PUBLIC RELATIONS
	Self-Righteous	Self-Serving	Self-Absorbed
	Criticism, Harshness	People Pleasing	Image Management
	IS THREATENING	IS WEAK	IS MANIPULATIVE
BEHAVIOR:	Self-Righteous Judgment —Slander —Presumption —Impatience	Enablement —Gossip —Guilt Trips —Martyr Complex	Spin (Spin Club) —Distorts, Redefines Truth —Political Intimidation —Victim of Circumstances
THE PROBLEM:	PRIDE	FEAR	DECEITFULNESS
THE ANTIDOTE:	HUMILITY	COURAGE	HONESTY

THE
PEOPLE MODEL
WORKBOOK

The purpose of the workbook is to equip you to lead in everyday situations. Every question is intended to assist both you and your group in your leadership and character development. Most of the questions are personal and probing, though some of them invite you to discuss various aspects of the book. Almost every question is open-ended.

SESSION 1
Setting Up Your Small Group
The People Model Workbook can be used by individuals or small groups. It applies to businesses, families, civic clubs, governments, churches, etc.

The workbook questions can be answered

- *on your own (for convenience and privacy)*
- *prior to meeting with a group (so that everyone will be prepared to share)*

- *on the spot in community with a group (so that no one will
  have homework)*

The workbook is designed to be covered in nine separate one-hour sessions. Of course, it can be used in any way that fits the group's schedule.

Each section is comprised of open-ended questions. If one particular question evokes an especially good discussion, then the group may choose to focus exclusively on it for an entire session. Whatever the group decides is acceptable.

Note: If the small group includes more than twelve people, it might be best to divide into subgroups. When small groups get too big, the conversation changes because it's hard for the discussion to go deep.

Usually small groups run best when someone agrees to serve as the facilitator. The facilitator's job is to guide the group in decision making and to lead the group discussions. The facilitator is also responsible to create space for each person to contribute (if they'd like) and to prevent anyone (including the facilitator!) from accidentally dominating the discussion.

Facilitator Checklist:

____ 1. The group has chosen me to be the facilitator, and I have agreed to serve.

____ 2. The group agrees to meet either weekly or biweekly.

____ 3. The group has decided what time to start and end the sessions.

____ 4. The group has committed to complete the workbook together in ____ sessions.

____ 5. Each member has already read the book and taken the People Model test.

____ 6. The group has agreed for each member to bring prepared answers ____ or to allow each other to answer the questions "cold" ____. (Put a check in the blank that fits.)

____ 7. The group has decided to allow visitors to join them. Yes ____ No ____

_____ 8. Each member of the group is informed of when meetings are scheduled.

_____ 9. Each member knows where the meetings will take place.

_____10. All members have introduced themselves to the group.

Many of the workbook questions ask people to talk about themselves. The idea is for the group to support one another, not pressure one another. It's important also for members of the group to keep sensitive matters confidential. (That's why it's good to decide beforehand whether or not to welcome visitors.)

Finally, it's helpful if the facilitator previews all the questions, so that the group can stay on course as much as possible.

Opening Discussion

1. Which of the three categories best describes you? Which one describes you the least? Which tailor-made title do you like best? (See page 151.)

   _____

   _____

2. Are most members of your group primarily from the same category? If so, which one? To achieve a better balance of all three types, does the group want to add any members from the other two groups before starting the second session?

   _____

   _____

3. What point in this book impacted you most? What lines in the book did you find helpful? Was there anything with which you disagreed?

   _____

   _____

4. Do you agree or disagree with the categorizations of famous Strategists, Humanitarians, and Diplomats on page 16?

   _____

   _____

5. Which character in the story do you relate to most and why?

_____

_____

6. Consider the situation at WeServTech. Have you seen a similar scenario play out at your own workplace? If so, briefly describe the dynamics.

_____

_____

7. Were you surprised to learn at the end that Nathan had been named president of another company? Why or why not?

_____

_____

SESSION 2
Seeing the People Model in Everyday Life

1. Refer back to the People Model Test. Do your observers' evaluations reflect the same conclusions as your self-evaluation? Are there any discrepancies in the details of these evaluations? If so, what can you learn from that?

_____

_____

_____

2. Which People Model category best fits your supervisor? Does your supervisor see himself or herself primarily in the same category in which you see him or her?

_____

_____

_____

3. Which category best describes your organization? How can supervisors develop those workers who are *not* of the same type that the organization tends to be overall? For instance, if your organization tends to award Humanitarians the most (for being loyal and agreeable), then how might it develop the Strategists

(who may seem threatening) and the Diplomats (who may seem to be manipulative)?

_____

_____

4. Think of those family members and friends with whom you are closest (spouse, children, parents, best friend or roommate). Which category best describes each of them?

_____

_____

5. Can you identify any points of conflict that might have arisen between you and your supervisor, or you and a family member, that the People Model chart can explain?

_____

_____

6. Name one problem that your organization is trying to address right now.

_____

   a. Is the company taking a Strategist approach and correcting it, or a Humanitarian approach and putting a short-term bandage on it, or a Diplomat approach and covering it up?

   _____

   _____

   b. How do you feel about what the company is doing with this problem?

   _____

   _____

   c. How many corrections do you think an organization or person can handle in any given period of time? How do you know when it's better to address problems with short-term solutions? How do you know when it's better to address problems cosmetically rather than to address them at the root?

   _____

   _____

7. Do people in your organization believe that there is such a thing as objective truth? Or would they argue instead that you have your truth and they have theirs? What did you think of John Mark's comment, "Everyone knows what truth is because everybody knows how to lie"? (See page 56.)

_____

_____

_____

SESSION 3
Going Deeper with Yourself

1. What are your strongest qualities *above* the line? What qualities do your coworkers or group members consider to be your strongest?

_____

_____

2. Where do you most tend to fall *below* the line? Where do those with whom you work see you falling into the basement? Have you asked them for their honest opinions?

_____

_____

3. What character qualities do you most desire to develop? For example, if you're primarily a Strategist, you may want to be more refined and empathetic. If you're primarily a Humanitarian, you may want to learn to be more confrontational and yet more sensitive to timing. If you're a Diplomat, you may want to become more accountable and compassionate.

_____

_____

4. Which trap are you most likely to fall into: that of being cynical, feeling guilty, or being aloof?

_____

_____

5. *Cynicism* is a form of anger and despair. Strategists are susceptible to becoming cynical when truthfulness is devalued and
   promises are broken.

   a. It hurts to be rejected when you're pointing out an aspect of
      the truth. Have you ever felt rejected for telling the truth?
      Can you tell a quick story about it?

      _____

      _____

   b. What happens to an organization (or a marriage) when truth
      is persistently ignored?

      _____

      _____

   c. What is the antidote to cynicism?

      _____

      _____

6. There are two kinds of guilt—true guilt and false guilt. True
   guilt arises when a person really *is* guilty of something. True
   guilt is an element above the line in the Strategists' category.
   False guilt is a by-product of fear. False guilt arises when a
   person feels guilty about something he or she is not responsible
   for. False guilt is an element below the line in the Humanitarians' category.

   a. Are you carrying a sense of guilt about something? Do you
      feel guilty for not pleasing a certain person? What does that
      person expect from you? Are those expectations realistic?

      _____

      _____

   b. What is the antidote to feeling guilt ridden?

      _____

      _____

   c. What is the antidote to people pleasing?

      _____

      _____

7. To be *aloof* is to be overly detached from other people. To be aloof is to be too focused on oneself or one's own interests. Diplomats have a tendency to retreat from other people and be isolated or emotionally inaccessible. Aloofness can also be described as an inappropriate form of self-protectiveness. Aloofness allows a person to hide, even from himself or herself.

a. Have you ever realized that you were deceiving yourself? How did you find out about it?

_____

_____

b. Have you ever felt trapped in your self-image? In other words, have you ever felt as though you *couldn't* tell people that you were struggling because it would wreck your core sense of identity? _____

_____

c. What is the antidote to aloofness?

_____

_____

SESSION 4
Becoming a Better Strategist

1. What are your strongest Strategist attributes (both above and below the line)?

_____

_____

2. Whom do you tend to be most judgmental of? Whom do you most often critique? What seems to try your patience the most? Why is it hard for you to withstand the process of waiting on *that* particular thing? What's at stake?

_____

_____

3. You've heard the old saying to "take the log out of your own eye before you remove the speck from someone else's." What does

that mean? How can your organization (or family) be more truthful? How can it become less hypocritical?

_____

_____

4. Can you think of a current situation in which Strategists are attacking other Strategists? What will it take to get them to stop fighting? What does the People Model suggest?

_____

_____

5. Review pages 107–108. In what ways are you tempted to attempt to turn the stones into bread in your workplace? in your family?

_____

_____

6. Sometimes people would rather have a magic genie than worship a God whose ways are hard to understand. Have you ever been angry at God for not turning the stones into bread, that is, for *not* doing exactly what you prayed that he would do? Have you ever experienced God's comfort?

_____

_____

_____

7. In what specific ways would you like to become a better Strategist? How can you be a humble Strategist?

_____

_____

SESSION 5
Becoming a Better Humanitarian

1. What are your strongest Humanitarian attributes (both above and below the line)?

_____

_____

2. Whose disapproval do you most fear? Whom do you tend to be most afraid to confront? Is it easier for you to confront someone else? Who? What makes it easier or harder for you to confront someone?

_____

_____

_____

3. How do other people feel when the leader of the company enables someone to work below the line?

_____

_____

_____

4. Review pages 108–109. In what ways are you tempted to bow down to the status quo in your workplace? in your family?

_____

_____

_____

5. Can you think of a current situation in which Humanitarians are enabling someone else? What will get them to stop? What does the People Model suggest?

_____

_____

_____

6. Do you feel prompted to do something that you fear may upset someone whom you're trying to please? Explain.

_____

_____

_____

7. In what ways would you like to be a better Humanitarian? How can you develop into a courageous Humanitarian?

_____

_____

_____

SESSION 6

Becoming a Better Diplomat

1. What are your strongest Diplomat qualities (both above and below the line)?

   _____

   _____

2. Whom are you trying most to impress? Why do you want to impress them?

   _____

   _____

3. Review page 107. In what ways are you tempted to show off?

   _____

   _____

4. How do people feel when the leader of your organization redefines the truth instead of admitting it openly? Have you ever seen that happen? If so, how did you feel about it?

   _____

   _____

5. Can you think of a situation in which Diplomats are currently leading below the line? What will it take to motivate them to stop? What does the People Model suggest?

   _____

   _____

   _____

6. Consider the Solutions Chart (see page 158). Give an example of what it means to nuance your remarks.

   _____

   _____

7. In what specific ways would you like to become a better Diplomat? How can you develop into an honest Diplomat?

   _____

   _____

SESSION 7
Finding Help to Rise above the Line

1. Who is the most above-the-line leader you can think of? What makes him or her a model leader?

   _____

   _____

   _____

2. Although the People Model has no power to transform a person's character, it can still guide someone who wants to make positive changes in his or her life. Consider this: Sometimes it takes a bank shot to get yourself back into the upstairs of your primary category.

   If a Diplomat, for instance, wants to rise out of the Diplomat basement, one way to do that is to aim for the Humanitarian upstairs by making it a point to serve others. Serving other people may help the Diplomat to be less self-absorbed.

   Similarly, a Humanitarian may rise out of the Humanitarian basement by aiming for the clarity of the Strategist upstairs. When a Humanitarian is stuck in the basement, feeling anxious or guilty, he or she cannot think clearly because negative emotions of fear and guilt interfere with his or her clarity of thought.

   Likewise, a Strategist in the basement may rise above the line by aiming for the calmness of a Diplomat. Calmness helps a person to wait and withhold judgment.

   Which bank shot do you most need to make?

   _____

   _____

   _____

3. Everyone feels angry sometimes. Using the People Model chart, describe how a Strategist might express anger. How about a Humanitarian? a Diplomat?

   _____

   _____

   _____

4. What kind of help do you need in order to rise above the line in your leadership? in your relationships with your coworkers? in your relationships outside of work?

_____

_____

5. How might God help you as you attempt to lead above the line more consistently?

_____

_____

SESSION 8
The Power of the People Model

1. Since reading *Leadership above the Line*, which of the three powers—explanatory, motivational, or creative—have you exercised in your workplace or personal life at home? Explain.

_____

_____

2. Using the explanatory power of the People Model, explain why Strategists tend to be so tied to their own opinions while honest Diplomats do not.

_____

_____

3. Using the motivational power of the People Model, describe how a Humanitarian could begin to break the habit of people pleasing.

_____

_____

4. Using the creative power of the People Model, explain a good way to stay above the line if your supervisor asks you to do something unethical.

_____

_____

5. Share your response to the challenges on pages 157–158 with your small group.

SESSION 9
Staying above the Line

1. What in this workbook impacted you most?

_____

_____

_____

2. What were the highlights of your small group experience?

_____

_____

_____

3. Have you noticed any changes in your behavior since beginning the study? any transformation in your character?

_____

_____

_____

4. In what ways have you applied the People Model? How has the Solutions Chart helped you?

_____

_____

_____

5. Although this is not a book on mentoring, John Mark and Lisa's relationship illustrates how a beneficial mentoring relationship can work. Is there anyone within your group with whom you can keep meeting as you both seek to stay above the line?

_____

_____

_____

ABOUT
THE AUTHOR

Dr. Sarah Sumner serves as special assistant to the dean for strategic development and as professor of theology and ministry in the Haggard School of Theology at Azusa Pacific University. She graduated from Baylor University and Wheaton College with a goal to write books, travel, and speak. Having earned a doctorate in systematic theology from Trinity Evangelical Divinity School and an MBA from Azusa Pacific, she is now a seasoned teacher and published author of *Men and Women in the Church: Building Consensus on Christian Leadership* (InterVarsity Press, 2003) and *Leadership above the Line* (Tyndale, 2006). Dr. Sumner travels extensively as a keynote speaker and consultant. She also serves as a regular teaching pastor at New Song Church in San Dimas, California, and as an aerobics instructor at Bally Total Fitness. She and her husband, Jim, enjoy taking long walks together and doing the East Coast Swing on the dance floor. Currently, they're writing a book on marriage and hoping to adopt an older child.